Michael & Lili,

with love,

Tommy

Mobilizing Commitment

Facilitating Organizational Transformation through Dialogue

THOMAS F. GROSS

To order additional copies of this book, contact:
Xlibris Corporation
1-888-795-4274
www.Xlibris.com
Orders@Xlibris.com
87076

Contents

Preface

The background for the creation of this book began in 1990 when I moved my consulting practice from the USA to Geneva, Switzerland and founded Genesis Consulting Group. I had decided to focus my practice on the dynamic market for corporate change which had been catalyzed by the creation of the European Union. Corporations were taking advantage of new, open markets by integrating national entities into European and Global structures as well as acquiring and merging with other corporations. I was attracted to the dynamism of multi-national, multi-cultural organizational change. I was also fulfilling a life-long passion of visiting and working in different countries, having lived and worked in both Latin America and Europe earlier in life while learning both Spanish and German. I created Genesis as a pan-European partnership with consultants from Germany, Sweden, France, the Netherlands and the UK whom I had come to know through consulting collaborations. The business goal coincided with the personal goal which my wife and I had had for our family. The move to Europe would afford our three children the opportunity to learn foreign languages and cultures first hand.

Over the years, the original partners left Genesis and new ones joined until the current configuration gelled: Kees Bultink and Arri Pauw from the Netherlands, Michael Manolson from Canada and I from the USA. Kees joined Genesis in 1994. He and I had collaborated earlier, from 1989-1994, when I was the external consultant with GE Plastics Europe and Kees was the internal consultant, serving as head of Quality Assurance. Together, Kees and I had tailored and delivered a cross functional team-based, meeting methodology across Europe called Workout! Chairman Jack Welch conceived the process to change the culture of GE by supporting rapid problem solving across organizational boundaries both up and down the hierarchy and horizontally across divisions, departments and geographies. He intended to open the culture from too much top autocracy and counterproductive internal friction.

Together, individually and with sub-contractors, Kees and I facilitated hundreds of GE Workout! meetings in at least 15 European countries. We also designed and delivered a facilitator training program to over 1000 GE managers which supported the organization in developing its own capabilities in delivering Workout! meetings. Kees and I went on to support Novartis Pharmaceuticals for several years in tailoring and delivering the Novartis modification of GE's Workout!, called FAR (Fast Action for Results) across multiple divisions and multiple geographies around the world.

Arri Pauw joined Genesis in 1994. Arri and I had collaborated since 1993 when I was the external consultant and Arri was the VP Human Resources in one of the Unilever divisions. After Arri became a partner, he and I facilitated the integration of that Unilever division from a federation of national European companies into one, integrated European organization. We went on to facilitate the merger integration of that same division with a multi-national company which Unilever had acquired, resulting in its transformation from a European to a global entity. Over the next several years we provided similar consultant support to various Unilever divisions in Europe and Latin America especially those that were integrating national entities into single regional entities.

In 1996, Arri, Kees and I compiled the tools and concepts we had been using into the Genesis Methodology and Toolkit. Our collaborative, dialogue-centered approach to facilitating organizational transformation was codified for the first time as an internal publication. Since then, we have built upon and continued to develop our methodology. This book represents another iteration in that continuous process.

Arri and I were serving as external consultants in the development of the Earth Center, a new not-for-profit theme park in the UK devoted to educating the public on conservation and sustainable economic development in 1999. It was there we met Michael Manolson, who was on their staff. Michael had recently left his position as Chief Executive of Greenpeace, Canada. After Michael joined Genesis in 2000, he collaborated with us partners on a range of consulting projects while learning the Genesis approach experientially.

From its inception in 1990 through the early 2000s Genesis expanded and contracted in terms of numbers of partners several times and has continued to evolve. Each of the four of us has developed his own consulting practice in his own manner while retaining the Genesis foundation of values and methodology. Kees has focused on manufacturing clients and became certified as a Six Sigma black belt instructor. Kees integrates the Genesis dialogue centered, collaborative approach with Six Sigma quality improvement change processes. Arri incorporates Gestalt methodology principles. His approach now integrates coaching with leaders and the strengthening of relationships within the context of comprehensive organizational change. In addition, Arri has developed a leadership development program (see http://genesisleadership.org) focused on self-awareness. Michael supports a number of global divisions of multinationals in the development and deployment of global strategies around the world. He is also the member of several boards of directors of not-for-profit organizations devoted to community well-being. In addition to corporate consulting, I have become involved in consulting and executive coaching with not-for-profit organizations in the fields of conservation, sustainable economic development, philanthropy and international understanding.

This book strives to describe how we work to fulfill our mission as a firm: " . . . to partner with, support and coach leaders in the process of transforming their organizations to strengthen implementation and results. The process we employ involves and mobilizes people across the organization, from the leadership team to the front line, with shared understanding, ownership and commitment."

It has had three purposes. First, the process of writing this book, including all of the discussions and multiple drafts, has supported my partners and me in refining our practice and learning from one another as partners. Secondly, the book is designed to serve facilitators, including leaders as well as internal and external consultants, who are striving to mobilize commitment to transformation and strengthen organizational effectiveness and results. Finally, the writing of the book has helped me clarify and stimulate my continuing journey of learning as a facilitator of change.

The first section of the book presents the principles and methods which guide our work. They have their roots in the fields of organizational psychology, Gestalt methodology and systems theory. They are illustrated with examples from the cases to follow (Section 2), as well as with vignettes from other consulting projects of mine. In recent years I have been receiving training and coaching in Gestalt therapy. The Gestalt perspective and self awareness have helped me look back on our Genesis experience with new lenses. Gestalt has broadened my understanding of the process of dialogue, particularly with regard to the importance of awareness. There are at least three classes of dialogue we have employed which are essential for change. In our coaching role we support our client-leaders in gaining self awareness on their behavior through inner dialogue. In both our coaching and facilitating roles we support the development of trusting relationships, especially in leadership teams, through relational dialogue. In our facilitation role we support the development of solutions and implementation through strategic dialogue in leadership teams. Inner dialogue, relational dialogue and strategic dialogue are the inter-related means by which leaders of organizational transformation gain awareness of what needs to be done and how to do it; mobilize commitment across their organizations and implement organizational transformation.

The second section presents detailed accounts of representative cases of our work with leaders and their organizations. The case material is selected to represent what in Genesis we identify as three levels of facilitation: mobilizing commitment through the macro process across the entire organization; dialogue in meetings; and moments of awareness. The first two cases relate to the macro process. The first one, *Long-term Improvement (Chapter 11)*, was facilitated by Arri Pauw. The second case, *Globalization (Chapter 12)*, was facilitated by Michael Manolson. The next two cases relate to the meeting. The third case, *Accelerated strategy development (Chapter 13)*, was facilitated by Kees Bultink. The fourth case, *Merger Integration* (Chapter 14) was facilitated by me with some support from Kees and Michael and another consultant, as well. The examples which relate to facilitating moments are selected from the case material and are illustrated in the chapter which addresses the relationship of the three levels of facilitation, *Chapter 5, Fractals: moments of shared awareness, meetings of dialogue and macro processes which mobilize commitment*. We had wanted to share the names of the clients and their companies in this book yet we were deterred by the confidentiality concerns. We settled on fictitious names.

We hope our collective Genesis story supports your journey as a facilitator of organizational transformation in large and complex organizations like multinational corporations, whether you are a leader or an internal or external consultant.

Acknowledgements

This book was born out of conversations with my Genesis partners, Arri Pauw, Kees Bultink and Michael Manolson. I am indebted to them for their colleagueship and friendship and the support they have given to me over the years of writing this book. I had proposed to them that we write a book on our consulting practice in order to stimulate learning from one another and enrich our individual approaches. Initially I served as the journalist and wrote the four cases, one from each of us, which served as the foundation material for this book. We talked about the cases on multiple occasions until we were satisfied with their accuracy and we had learned what each of us had done in those cases and why.

Arri tirelessly reviewed and commented on multiple drafts of this book throughout the writing process. My dear friend and business partner of over seventeen years, the legacy of our collaboration is present throughout this book. Arri consistently stimulates my learning and growth as a practitioner and as a person. He encouraged me to think of this book, not only as a Genesis book, but as my book. I took the challenge and put more of my own voice and personal reflections into the writing.

Kees and Michael have also generously shared with me their feedback throughout the course of the writing of the book. The collaboration on consulting projects I have enjoyed with each of them is also deeply embedded in this book.

After several years of conversation with Arri, Kees and Michael and countless drafts I hit the wall. I found it difficult to organize with clarity the writing of the tools we use, the underlying psychological principles and the illustrations from the case material. I decided I needed help to get through the block from outside the circle of my Genesis partners.

I joined a writers' workshop, led by Joe Melnick, a therapist, coach, writer, editor and organizational consultant at the Gestalt International Study Center (GISC), Wellfleet, Massachusetts, where I had previously taken several programs. Joe's support in that workshop and over the succeeding months was instrumental in re-stoking my enthusiasm to find new insights and freshness in the writing and also include more of my personal voice and experience.

I learned that blocks to achieve self-professed goals are not uncommon. As I had instinctively thought in joining Joe's meeting, I discovered that a key to overcoming my writing block was getting new support. He also suggested that I enlist friends and other colleagues in reading drafts and giving me feedback. Nervously, I did it. The substantive feedback has been important and my energy has been stimulated by the involvement of people I like, trust and respect. In the terms of the Gestalt cycle of experience, as taught at GISC, this book has been the phase of making meaning for me on several decades of professional work.

Edwin Nevis, a founder of GISC, has broadened my understanding of the process of moments of awareness in organizational transformation and repeatedly challenged me to put more of my personal experiences into the writing through writing in the first person. His writings and the programs which I have taken at GISC have helped me reflect back on my practice and deepen my understanding of the relationship of dialogue to awareness and organizational transformation.

Chris Argyris was my dissertation advisor more than thirty years ago. From Chris I learned that powerful learning and personal behavior change come with disciplined reflection on one's own experience. His innovative approach to action research whereby he has studied his own consulting interventions became the model for the writing of this book, as it was earlier for the writing of my dissertation. I began with the data—the case material from my partners and me. From there, I worked to reflect on those experiences and produce the first section of the book, the principles and methods. The body of Chris's work on organizational behavior and learning is one of the sources of my own ideas on dialogue on which my consulting approach is based. Chris also generously read a near final draft and provided me with invaluable suggestions and challenges to reveal my thinking as a consultant.

My friends and colleagues, John Aber, John Diliberti, Mauricio Goldstein, Helen Goodman, Ron Innerfield, Meredith Jones, Talia Levine Bar-Yoseph, Charlie McMillan, Pete and Emily Morfin, Joel Pasternack, Ellen Pope, Cecilia Rodriguez, Dan Stork, Zeynep Tozum and Wolfgang Vieten, took the time to read my manuscript and offer me their candid feedback, helped me clarify my writing and delete the extraneous and emphasize the more interesting.

My wife, Maria and my children, Abby, Adam and Naomi, have listened to my stories throughout my consulting career and joined me on our great family adventure of moving to Europe so I could start up Genesis. Adam, a graphics designer, designed the cover. Maria has been my greatest supporter every step of the way, including as editor of the final draft of the book.

Thank you, dear friends, colleagues and family.

Thomas F. Gross
Center Conway, New Hampshire

Section 1
Principles and Methods for
Leading Organizational Transformation

Chapters
1. Foundation: trusting relationships
2. Means: strategic and relational dialogue
3. Goal: mobilizing commitment
4. Barriers: different perceptions, different realities
5. Fractals: moments of shared awareness, meetings of dialogue and macro processes which mobilize commitment
6. Boundaries: experiencing freedom within a framework
7. Multiplier affects: leveraging total resources and strengthening individual capability and performance
8. Scope: transforming the entire system
9. Discovery: action learning
10. Conclusion

Chapter 1
Foundation: Trusting Relationships

The manufacturing VP and four of his subordinates, all factory managers, had agreed on a productivity improvement program. I had facilitated the planning process. During the first phase of implementation I received an irate email from one of the factory managers, Hal. He reported that one of the other factory managers, Jasper, had made an expenditure on new equipment without consulting the group. Hal had thought he and his colleagues had agreed to make these decisions collaboratively. My first reaction was disappointment and nervousness that the hard work of the clients was in danger of unraveling. I also felt initial anger toward Jasper for acting independently and was tempted to write him a challenging email. I caught myself. I reminded myself that in my role as facilitator I needed to remain neutral in the conflict. I also worried that I may have contributed to the conflict inadvertently by not having helped them develop a more thorough plan in the first place.

I decided to return to the factual record of the work we had done together. I reviewed the document which summarized their productivity improvement plan. I found nothing to substantiate that Jasper had violated the agreement. Hal's understanding, which I had almost shared, was implicit. There was nothing in writing that financial expenditure decisions regarding the program would be made by all four plant managers together.

I spoke with each of the four plant managers individually to understand more completely their views on what had just occurred and invite them to meet together again. Hal explained to me with passion that he believed that Jasper, Tim, Martin and he had agreed, in spirit, that these kinds of decisions would be shared among the four plant managers even though it was not in writing. The heat increased as the other two factory managers, Tim and Martin, agreed with Hal. I first listened and then asked each one how they wanted to proceed. The productivity program was in jeopardy. Hal, Tim and Martin were considering telling their boss, the manufacturing VP, that they could not work with Jasper. I explored with each of them what the consequences of that approach would be for each, individually, and for the company. They each acknowledged they all had more potentially to gain if they tried to resolve the conflict before going to the boss. They each agreed to give it a try.

When we got together, the anger was still high on the part of each of the four. Jasper felt justified in making the expenditure while the other three reiterated that they thought that Jasper had violated their agreement. I asked them to return to their agreed productivity improvement plan and pinpoint which aspects either demonstrated that Jasper had violated the agreement or supported his interpretation that he was within his rights to have acted independently. Hal, Tim and Martin acknowledged that there were no clauses which Jasper had violated. Yet, once again, they maintained that Jasper had violated the "partnership spirit" of the agreement.

I suggested to the four that since they had such different perceptions that they return to the planning process and develop a more comprehensive plan, which would cover more contingencies and avoid future misunderstandings. I explained that in my experience, plans on complex issues with much at stake frequently required multiple iterations of development until all parties were satisfied that ambiguities and different points of interpretation had been clarified. I hoped the exercise of having another iteration of plan development and refinement would also be a useful learning experience. The four agreed without enthusiasm.

After a hiatus of a month, the four plant managers returned to the planning table. We began when I asked them what values should guide the development of their new plan. The principle of "fair and equitable access to resources" was agreed. I also asked them what was at stake for each of them personally. They acknowledged that their careers would be affected by the outcome of the productivity improvements which they planned and implemented.

I then asked them why the issue had sparked such anger among them. They acknowledged that the conflict had been born out of competitive feelings for one another. They next began to share that they were shifting their view. They now felt that collaboration would more likely assure a positive outcome for each of them. If they continued to be in conflict, they feared that it could result in negative evaluations for some or all of the four by their boss, the V.P.; furthermore, they would not be able to realize the full potential of the productivity improvement program. The meeting resulted in a commitment to develop their next productivity improvement plan based on the values of equity, partnership and collaboration.

I felt relieved. The four plant managers had moved away from a conflict which had threatened the collapse of their work and my work with them. It could have led to a long lasting fissure in the relationship between Jasper and his three colleagues. Instead, Jasper and his three fellow plant managers had begun to restore trust in their relationships. And I felt that I was also maintaining trust with each of them. I hoped and believed that their next effort at planning would be more complete and of higher quality than their first plan.

Trusting relationships

The foundation of transforming an organization lies in trusting relationships first among the leaders and over time across the entire organization.

Professional colleagues, like mountain climbers tethered to the same rope as they scale a rock face, depend upon one another. When they take their first climb together, they begin with trust based on what they know of each other's experience and reputation and how they plan and prepare their first climb together. Their trust begins to build as they experience each other's openness and honesty regarding their mutual readiness for the climb: physically, technically and emotionally. As they begin their climb, they learn to deepen their trust in one another through the experience of taking risks, finding each other responsive, competent, consistent, reliable and capable of learning and recovering from mistakes.

As they execute the climb they encounter challenging puzzles to solve. With awareness, which mobilizes energy, they choose the next moves. With each success they relax for a moment and perhaps smile before beginning the cycle anew. They learn to improve working together by giving one another feedback in the moment, when it is urgent and feedback when they have time to reflect on the totality of what each did during the climb. Through experience, they learn to support one another physically, technically and emotionally and to feel safe with one another. Over time, they take on more challenging climbs.

Each step of completion builds competence and trust in one another, themselves individually and together as a team. Completion and trust building occur on different time scales: at the end of a difficult move within a climb, at the end of a climb, at the end of an expedition which includes a series of climbs and over the years, after a variety of expeditions.

We will now examine a case where the deficit in trust was less personal and more systemic than the situation with the four factory managers. In this example, disparate units in a company were being told by senior management to integrate their operations. The managers of the units did not trust that the process would serve their interests and initially resisted. This was Michael's work with the purchasing division of the MNX (fictitious name) corporation.

Examples of trusting relationships as a foundation for transformation from Genesis cases (Section 2)

Michael worked closely with the lead manager, the Vice President of Global Purchasing, Division I, of the "MNX" Corporation over a period of six years (Chapter 12, Globalization). Together, Michael facilitated and his client, the Vice President, whom we shall call Ludwig, led the process of strengthening collaboration and integration among previously fragmented regional Purchasing Units in order to deliver significant cost savings. The process comprised a series of meetings led by Ludwig, facilitated by Michael and included the members of Ludwig's management team. Michael preceded each meeting by interviewing each member of the management team. The interview data were synthesized by Michael into issues for the team to address and if necessary, decide upon. The agendas for the meetings were designed by Michael in consultation with Ludwig and were based on the interview syntheses.

Ludwig and Michael had already worked together in the client-consultant relationship successfully and had developed trust in one another. Ludwig recognized that his challenge required the skills of facilitating dialogue and process. He knew Michael had these skills and he did not. He anticipated that his colleagues would resist working with him. He was taking on the job with his eyes wide open. He came from a background outside of purchasing and he expected that some of his new colleagues would feel he could not understand their work. He would not have line authority over the team; instead, he was appointed as a peer with the job of project manager. Decisions would need to be made by consensus. He expected that decision making would be difficult.

Ludwig also knew that many of his new colleagues were explicitly averse to the overall goal to globalize their operations. Each one was a lead buyer in one of the major regions of the world and enjoyed considerable power, autonomy and the perks that came with the authority to make decisions involving huge sums of money. They would now be expected to relinquish some control over their regional operations and share the purchasing process with colleagues in other regions. Previously, these units had overtly not trusted one another. While they were all part of the global function of corporate purchasing, before the integration process, they had never coordinated with one another to achieve economies of scale. While the regional buyers understood that the senior management decision to globalize was clear and the significant cost savings benefits to MNX were obvious to all, their emotional resistance nonetheless was high.

In the process of designing their new organization, via the series of meetings, Ludwig and Michael opened the discussion early on to these concerns. The individual buyers gave voice to their resistance in the initial meetings. The openness resulted in a shared awareness that all buyers were concerned in similar ways that they might be hurt by the proposed integration. The shared awareness helped mobilize the team to proceed with the integration discussions and diminished their sense of rivalry with one another. They had begun to articulate that while previously they had not known each other, and perhaps had not trusted each other, now they were working together and their prior feelings were giving way to a feeling of collaboration and trust.

By contributing to the process, they were also able to discuss the barriers to establishing the global supplier organization which came from outside the circle of regional buyers. Each had a direct reporting relationship to a boss in the home region. While all of the bosses in their regional organizations publicly supported the establishment of Global Purchasing, some privately opposed the idea. In at least one instance a regional purchasing manager had been instructed by his superior to ignore global targets and focus only on delivering regional targets. This dilemma also was shared in the new team and the manager received support from his colleagues to help his superior understand that corporate leadership was clear, global targets could not and would not be ignored.

In the meetings, the new team of regional purchasing managers also shared their resentment of what they perceived as contradictory messages from senior management: "globalize, but . . ." MNX had already taken significant steps to globalize marketing, R&D, HR and other functions. Purchasing resided within the manufacturing organization and MNX was slow to globalize manufacturing. Manufacturing was not given a seat with the Senior Leadership Team which ran MNX. The Regional Presidents, who were members of the MNX Senior Leadership Team, were the opponents. They wanted to continue to control manufacturing within each of their respective regions, ostensibly in order to control all elements of the P/L statements for which they were being held accountable. Consequently, the regional purchasing managers were told on the one hand, "globalize" and on the other hand, "your parent organization, manufacturing, will remain regionalized."

By openly exploring all of these obstacles in the meetings Ludwig, with Michael's support, worked collaboratively with his new colleagues and progressively gained their trust. The first five years of the integration process were devoted only to the globalization of the Purchasing organization in Division I, one of MNX's two global Divisions. Step by step, the process unfolded successfully. Other managerial levels from around the world began to collaborate first in meetings and then in day to day business. The meetings helped the managers get to know each other, begin to trust each other and to bring down costs by collaboratively developing their plans. In the fifth year, based on that success, MNX's senior management decided to integrate the purchasing operations of Division I with the purchasing operations of Division II, MNX's second global Division. Michael supported that integration process as well. Ludwig was appointed the leader of the combined operations.

This integration project of Division I and Division II had been another step in MNX's continuing process to adapt its global organization to the competitive demands of the global economy. While in the past, senior management dicta had failed in other areas, this time it turned out to be different. Michael and Ludwig had been able to help the different units by employing the same approach they had used with Division I. Through a series of meetings, facilitated by Michael and led by Ludwig, they built trust and collaboration through dialogue grounded in openness and honesty. The targeted cost savings again were delivered.

Lessons in building trust

When contracting with the client leaders throughout the engagement, be explicit that one role you, as the facilitator will play is to support the building of trust in the leader's team through coaching and meeting facilitation. Get training as a coach so that you can support the clients to examine their relationships with one another, including the emotions they feel and the behaviors they employ which produce intentional and unintentional outcomes, both positive and negative.

By asking questions, support the client leaders to develop plans to experiment with new behaviors. In meetings, support them to discuss their most important issues, including positive and negative emotions such as those related to resistance. As the client leaders share with one another and their intimacy grows, their ability to collaborate on business issues will be enhanced.

From the outset of the engagement, diagnose relationships by assessing the levels of trust in the system and identifying breakdowns of communications between people or even overt conflict. Support team members to strengthen trust between and among themselves, as needed, through open exploration of difficult issues.

Be persistent, building trust can take time.

Chapter 2
Means: Strategic and Relational Dialogue

The four plant managers, Jasper, Hal, Tim and Martin reconvened to develop their productivity improvement plan one more time. This time they were clear. The plan would be grounded in a collaborative approach. Each of them committed that all resource allocation decisions pertaining to the program would be made by the four of them together, by consensus. That meant the majority would decide so long as the minority supported the decision after a healthy debate. There would be no more unilateral actions. This plan was more comprehensive than the first version. Their goals were also more ambitious. They began to see possibilities, especially by working together, where they could save money, collaborate on implementation and learn from one another. With greater trust as the foundation for their discussions, they created a productivity improvement plan about which they felt proud and their boss, the VP of manufacturing complemented as being significantly better than the first one they had developed some months earlier. He signed off on the new plan which cost more than the first plan yet promised a greater return on the investment.

My facilitation job had shifted. Instead of helping resolve conflict in relationships, I facilitated the dialogue concerning the development of a complex plan. The four plant managers negotiated openly, with attention to detail. They affirmed the value of equity. To confirm their agreement, they each signed the final document.

Strategic and relational dialogue

Strategic dialogue is the means for making sound decisions that are implemented and produce results.
It is characterized by two-way communication. While the goal is rationality grounded in facts, the parties recognize that their different beliefs and emotions can lead to different interpretations of the facts. This is a fundamental dimension of respect. They actively listen and are open to and curious about one another's different perspectives and feelings. They also voice their own perspectives and feelings clearly and with advocacy. They engage together in a process of discovering underlying assumptions, facts, emotions and ultimately solutions. The interactive process of sharing different viewpoints generates creativity, as the Hal/Jasper/Tim/Martin story reveals. They strive for shared understanding and awareness, ownership and commitment among all the parties. The hierarchy is maintained to expedite the decisions and their implementation. While the leader ultimately decides, the leader also considers the input of the team. The entire team takes their joint decisions as contracts with one another. Trust is enhanced.

Relational dialogue is the means for strengthening trusting relationships
Relational dialogue is synergistic with strategic dialogue. Collaboration and trust enhance execution and the achievement of results. The converse is also true.
Relational dialogue entails two-way feedback between individuals. They each bring an attitude of empathy and authenticity to the discussion. They discover the emotional and substantive impact they have had on one another, including unintended impact. In the process they recognize that their different beliefs and emotions may have led to different interpretations, misunderstanding, conflict and hurt feelings. They learn better how, in the future, to have the impact which they intend to have. They experience intimacy, contact and trust with one another.

Relational and Strategic Dialogue are enabled by Inner Dialogue
Inner dialogue can result in enhanced self awareness and inform both relational and strategic dialogue. At the beginning of the story of Hal/Jasper/Tim/Martin I had felt initial anger at Jasper for acting independently and was tempted to write him a challenging email. As I reflected on my emotions I reminded myself of the neutral role I needed to maintain as the facilitator. I avoided the trap of being perceived as taking sides. My inner dialogue helped me maintain trust with Jasper and his colleagues. Through listening to each of the managers and acknowledging their feelings, I was able to persuade them to return to the strategic dialogue and re-write their plan more carefully so misunderstandings would be less likely to occur in the future.

Strategic Dialogue

Strategic dialogue is characterized by reason, analysis, creativity and problem solving in order to deliver results. It is applied to the work of the organization, such as setting direction, allocating resources, negotiating, planning initiatives and innovations, etc. In our experience, many management teams and organizations are weak in the skills and tools of strategic dialogue, even though getting things done is the focus of their attention; that is one reason they engage external facilitators.

By facilitating strategic dialogue, as our cases illustrate, we help clients build new organizations and strengthen existing ones. Organizational development and transformation requires extensive planning, decision making and implementation across the complex areas of culture, business processes, strategy and structure.

Leaders of organizations in search of improved results find decisions are too frequently unclear, prove faulty in execution and must be revisited and reformulated. They also find too many individuals hold back from expressing alternative or conflicting viewpoints either out of fear of superiors or as a function of a culture that emphasizes and prides itself on friendliness and collegiality and implicitly, conflict avoidance. The culture of many management teams is a paradox; they are results oriented and yet make decisions rapidly so that afterwards, team members admit that they didn't understand or didn't agree with those decisions. It ends with poor implementation and disappointing results. Clients in one of the multinationals with whom we have worked frequently lamented before working with Genesis that "only after the decision was taken in the meeting, would the debate begin." We offered them an alternative, what we have defined under the banner, the Consultative Consensus decision making model. Consultative Consensus represented a 180 degree shift from their culture and served as an important tool to help them transform themselves. We have found the same to be true with many of our clients.

Consultative Consensus Decision Making Model
To address these common dysfunctions, we propose at the outset of most strategic meetings with clients that they adopt the Consultative Consensus decision making model for the first meeting as an experiment to see how effective they find it. We ask their permission to facilitate within the framework of the model. In so doing, we help them learn the efficacy of the model by using it.

The purpose of Consultative Consensus decision making is to assure that each team member has a voice, understands, owns, is committed to and takes responsibility and accountability for decisions and expeditious implementation. Team decision making is enhanced when every team member contributes their knowledge and opinions and the leader is open to the input. Over the twenty year history of Genesis this decision making tool has proved helpful in virtually all projects with our clients. Clients express appreciation for the model since it fulfills both the need for dialogue and the need for clear decisions while respecting the hierarchy. They also express relief from what they report as years of endemic problems with decision making and follow through in their organizations.

In the airline industry, pilot error has dramatically declined through the application of these principles with the development of a cockpit decision making strategy called Cockpit Resource Management (CRM). "The impetus for CRM came from a large NASA study in the 1970s of pilot error; it concluded that many cockpit mistakes were attributable, at least in part, to the 'God-like certainty' of the pilot in command. If other crew members had been consulted (or forcefully spoke up), or if the pilot had considered other alternatives, then some of the bad decisions might have been avoided. As a result, the goal of CRM was to create an environment in which a diversity of viewpoints was freely shared. Unfortunately, it took a tragic crash in 1978 for airlines to implement the system," as Lehrer reports. On approach to land the plane, the pilot found the landing gear lights not on and he feared that the landing gear was not deploying. As he tried various means to deploy the landing gear, he circled the airport several times. He was so fixated on the landing gear lights that he ignored warnings from his flight engineer that they were running out of fuel. The plane crashed and ten people died. Investigators found that the landing gear had deployed and the lights did not appear due to a faulty circuit. The mantra of the CRM program is "see it, say it, fix it". In recent years, CRM has moved beyond the cockpit and into the operating room for the same reason. Errors in surgery have been reduced significantly when every individual in the operating room has the obligation to express concerns freely to the operating surgeon.

Through the interviews we conduct as precursors for leadership team meetings, the CEO, or other leader of the team, receives comprehensive feedback regarding concerns (and opportunities).

Consultative Consensus decision making begins with dialogue and healthy debate, both rational and emotional. Rationality by itself is insufficient in making decisions that result in commitment to implementation. Commitment is grounded in emotions. The integration of rationality and emotions in effective decision making is increasingly being documented by neurological research, as well as in organizational research by my partner, Arri Pauw and others. It is not common for management teams to understand and communicate their emotions with regard to a decision; the cultural norm is to focus on rationality. Yet in our experience, as team members learn to become emotionally self aware and use their emotions as data to inform their own preferences, the dialogue and healthy debate become more profound and contribute to more effective strategic group decisions.

In one example, a client management team of mine was debating whether or not to invest in evaluating the impact of some of their work. While they could not cogently argue against evaluation, and saw many potential benefits, I observed a drop in energy in the conversation and a lack of enthusiasm for deciding affirmatively. I asked: *I wonder if you could say how you feel emotionally about doing evaluation, rather than rationally?* With one exception, every member of the team reported discomfort and concern that the exercise would divert time and money from other organizational priorities while not necessarily providing clear results. The team concluded and the CEO agreed that evaluation would not be a priority at this time.

Once the dialogue and healthy debate have run their course and a majority opinion has clearly emerged, the next step is team consensus. Given the openness and the contributions from everyone on the team those with the minority view can say, "We've been heard and while we do not agree, we can and will support the majority." This may be expressed colloquially as "60% agreement and 100% commitment." In rare instances, a member with the minority view will conclude, "I cannot support the majority and here are my reasons, once again . . . . If the leader supports the majority then either I will be granted an exemption and not be required to implement the decision or I will leave the organization or team."

In a management team devoted to a regional integration of country organizations, one of the country managers was vociferous in opposition to the regional integration. He argued that he could not be held accountable for his country's business results unless he continued to control all functions, including manufacturing and R&D. As the dialogue continued, it became apparent that he was alone. The CEO, while understanding intellectually and being supportive of Consultative Consensus decision making while not yet practiced with it, continued to try to persuade and placate this country manager. Other management team members began to fidget.

I then intervened in an effort to support the CEO and the team in learning the Consultative Consensus decision making model by experiencing it to be a helpful tool. I reminded the CEO and the group that they had signed on to the Consultative Consensus model. It was clear that consensus had emerged and the CEO was in agreement. Their decision making model was not unanimity. And if one member could not accept the decision, the individual could leave the organization. The CEO reiterated his agreement with the process and looked piercingly at the oppositional country manager. In return, the country manager looked down and in a quiet voice said, "I agree."

The management team learned to employ the Consultative Consensus decision making model, by using it. First use was with my facilitation, as described here. Over time the CEO and his team employed the model on their own, as they reported to me.

The final step is the team leader's decision! The hierarchy is reinforced. The leader has three choices: agreement with the consensus; agreement with the minority; or a decision to pursue a third alternative, possibly further study. The leader does *not abdicate* decision making authority to the consensus process. Instead, the leader uses the consensus process as a contribution to his or her ultimate decision.

As Nevis, et al put it: "Strategic interactions (i.e., dialogue) are the ways in which individuals exchange influence when the goal is to accomplish a specific task. Here, the intent is to use hierarchical power and to be less concerned with equality. Achieving the goal is of first importance and, though connectedness is still desired, mutuality gives way to getting something done. Hierarchy is maintained by willingness to lead and a willingness to follow."

The principles of Consultative Consensus decision making are intended to reinforce the purpose and the steps.

The first one, "once a decision is made, each member commits to and implements the decision as agreed" makes explicit that decision making is only effective if it results in implementation.

The next, "a decision is not to be second guessed unless new information arises and the team decides to reopen the decision" addresses the all-too-common phenomenon that some organizations describe whereby "team members seem to forget what they have agreed."

The final one, "the team employs ongoing feedback mechanisms to monitor the implementation process after the meeting" places the emphasis on follow up and effective implementation.

DECISION MAKING
CONSULTATIVE CONSENSUS

PURPOSE	STEPS	PRINCIPLES
ALL TEAM MEMBERS • HAVE A VOICE • UNDERSTAND, OWN AND ARE COMMITTED TO THE TEAM'S DECISIONS • TAKE RESPONSIBILITY AND ACCOUNTABILITY FOR EXPEDITIOUS IMPLEMENTATION	1. **DIALOGUE AND HEALTHY DEBATE—RATIONAL AND EMOTIONAL** 2. **TEAM CONSENSUS:** MAJORITY OPINION AND THE MINORITY SAYS, "WE'VE BEEN HEARD AND WHILE WE DO NOT AGREE, WE CAN AND WILL SUPPORT THE MAJORITY"/ 60% AGREEMENT AND 100% COMMITMENT. 3. **THE TEAM LEADER DECIDES** EITHER BY AGREEING WITH THE CONSENSUS, AGREEING WITH THE MINORITY OR DECIDING A THIRD ALTERNATIVE, POSSIBLY FURTHER STUDY.	• ONCE A DECISION IS MADE, EACH MEMBER COMMITS TO AND IMPLEMENTS THE DECISION, AS AGREED! • A DECISION IS NOT TO BE SECOND GUESSED UNLESS NEW INFORMATION ARISES AND THE TEAM DECIDES TO RE-OPEN THE DECISION • THE TEAM EMPLOYS ONGOING FEEDBACK MECHANISMS TO MONITOR THE IMPLEMENTATION PROCESS AFTER THE MEETING. AND AGREE ANY NECESSARY REMEDIAL ACTION

G E N E S I S

At the outset of our strategic meetings with clients, we expand what we mean by the first step, dialogue and healthy debate—rational and emotional. We propose four inter-related behaviors which characterize strategic dialogue: listen to others' and voice one's own ideas and emotions; make implicit assumptions explicit and decide which existing or new assumptions to employ; and respect one another. These we call Ground rules for Strategic Dialogue and they have evolved over the years from our own experience and from the literature. Our clients frequently report that they have already heard these ground rules and initially receive them as clichés, to be ignored. Yet, as we describe the desired behaviors in detail and we facilitate to help our clients manifest these behaviors, they gain awareness of the benefits of following the ground rules.

Ground rules for Strategic Dialogue
Suggestions for every member of a team

Listen to understand the other person's ideas and emotions

- Start with where everyone is.

  At the beginning of the meeting "check in" with how you and your team mates are feeling emotionally and what everyone's wishes are for the discussion. This process helps everyone to establish contact with one another, may result in a modified agenda and strengthens ownership for the meeting about to occur.

- Scan the group.

  As the meeting unfolds be aware of what is being said by everyone and what is being communicated non-verbally. This balances the tendency to be focused on what you want to say.

- Paraphrase and segue/ build on what others have said.

  Repeat the words that colleagues have used, particularly on high energy and/or emotional subjects, and address those words. This helps maintain continuity in the discussion and contact among the participants.

- Ask probing questions.

  To enhance further contact between individuals in the group, each individual in the group asks at least one question, addressing the person by name and listening for an answer while noticing whether or not an answer is received.

- Be open to being influenced by what others have said.

  What some refer to as "generous listening" includes a mindset of being open to learning and being willing to change one's own position.

Voice your Ideas and Emotions

- Discuss what is important, difficult and risky with openness and honesty.

  There are no sacred cows. Underlying assumptions which have guided behavior heretofore are invited to be shared and explored and changed, as necessary. The interview process, which precedes a meeting, helps individuals and the team to get this kind of data on the table early in the macro process of change.

- Be willing to influence others without coercion.

Voice what is important to you with conviction and authentic emotion.

- Spotlight the difficult issues where people disagree.
  Learning and creativity come from the points of disagreement and friction.

- All debates are team debates; encourage the views of everyone.
  If a debate becomes polarized between two individuals, then invite the other members of the group to speak their minds on the question, as well. New insights, frequently based on new assumptions are shared. A consensus usually emerges when everyone weights in. New inputs will frequently reframe and usually help resolve the debate between the original two. The teams' bonds with one another are typically strengthened as a consequence of robust and healthy team debates.
  If some members are silent, perhaps because they are naturally introverted, invite their contributions. Each individual should intentionally take their share of time, no more and no less (regardless of being an introvert or extrovert).

Make Explicit what have been Implicit Assumptions

- Identify key words that people employ with different meanings and reconcile the differences.
  Recognize that we each view reality with somewhat different paradigms, (mental models and emotional habits) which shape our perceptions (Chapter 4, Barriers: different perceptions, different realities).

- Explore different meanings for the use of a given word, as an antidote to the destructive attitude that one is "right" and the other is "wrong".

- Formulate and test assumptions utilizing any or all of three approaches to help team members gain awareness (discussed below, in Chapter 5):
  o Ask questions to uncover assumptions, such as "why?"
  o Present a new "figure" of an assumption that you see, yet others may not yet see
  o Invite the team members to participate in a new experience, "an experiment", such as a role play

Once the group develops a shared awareness of an assumption it may be formulated and tested as a hypothesis for the group to explore. The process of *making the implicit explicit* helps support group learning, creativity and shared awareness.

Respect each Individual

- Establish a flat hierarchy during the dialogue; no pulling rank. The leader participates in the dialogue with opinions rather than decisions.
- The decision maker only decides after the dialogue and healthy debate is over.
- Dialogue requires an attitude of co-equality, what Buber referred to as the "I-thou" relationship.
- Hostility is out of bounds, either direct or indirect, such as hostile sarcasm.
- Avoid attributions of motives or evaluative statements since they tend to provoke defensiveness. Use "I" statements rather than "you" statements.

Relational dialogue

Relational dialogue is manifested by building trust, empathy and authenticity. These, in turn, are a result of the awareness of one's own emotions and the powerful influence which emotions have on one's own and others' behavior and decision making. It helps strengthen relationships by bringing people in contact with one another and when necessary, by resolving their conflicts.

"Intimate interactions are those that bring us closer to each other through caring about what each person is thinking or feeling," as Nevis, et al, state further. "The intent is to enhance connectedness as a desirable goal in its own right. The behavior is used as a way of being together in a mutually powerful way, whether the context is a couple, a family, or an organizational relationship."

While many organizations are weak in strategic dialogue, more are even weaker in relational dialogue. These organizations have cultures which are so focused on tasks and results that the importance of trusting relationships between organizational members is actually out of their awareness.

Business problems in these organizations are addressed with even more intense strategic focus, frequently with no better outcomes. Low trust in some critical relationships can actually impair results because of conflicts or simply poor collaboration. Not uncommon in large organizations is what my partner, Arri Pauw, refers to as "subtle sabotage", such as not answering an email from a colleague who is not trusted.

Managers in these cultures have little practice with what might be called "difficult conversations"—giving and receiving feedback on behavior to resolve conflict and optimize learning. Instead they frequently manifest avoidance of these difficult conversations. If the awareness of these relationship problems exists at all it is frequently coupled with the hope that the issues will be handled by the HR professionals.

In these organizations, processes only grounded in strategic dialogue are not sufficient. In order to raise the performance of the organization, the building and nurturing of trusting relationships through relational dialogue is also essential.

The CEO and head of marketing of yet another client company of mine, had not been talking for months. They each shared with me independently that the situation was difficult and painful and they were each disappointed in the other. The CEO asked me to mediate a conversation, a difficult conversation, between him and the head of marketing. The latter agreed. We booked a conference room over a period of a day and one half. Each shared their story of the relationship between the two, which was now over three years old. The CEO spoke of his pain in attending to a quality problem with a major customer over many months and which he had thought had been partly a function of the neglect by the head of marketing. The head of marketing spoke of his pain of being cut off from all communication with the CEO and how he had felt unfairly blamed.

The two had drifted apart and had not talked to each other constructively for months. Over the day and one half, they heard each other well and became aware that each had had unintended negative impacts on the other. They also became aware that they each contributed to the long silence in their relationship. Their mutual awareness generated positive energy to clarify further how the head of marketing could contribute to the organization in a new role and do that effectively in a new geographic location that was important to him. The conversation also included reflections on mutual successes and creative solutions to other difficult hurdles.

The process I employed represents one of the tools we teach clients to learn to improve their skills in building trust—ground rules for relational dialogue. It is the product of our own experience and input from many models employed to guide the giving of difficult feedback.

Ground Rules for Relational Dialogue

The goal is to provide two-way feedback so that both parties understand what the other has said and they establish contact with one another. Feedback to resolve conflict and optimize learning is characterized by strong emotions, positive or negative; such as gratitude or disappointment, appreciation or anger; joy or sadness, etc. Effective feedback is grounded in mutual respect meaning no blaming, shaming or hostility. This creates shared understanding, i.e., a shared perception or shared awareness of what happened and its impact on all parties. It results in positive energy in the relationship.

What happened?
- Describe behaviorally what occurred: what you and the other person said or what you both did with or to one another.
- The objective is that you both agree on what happened. Given the distorting filters that we each employ while remembering especially emotionally laden events, this process may require several iterations. I may think you said "X", while you think you said "Y". To come to an agreement over what happened may require that each of us concedes that we may not be remembering precisely the words that were spoken.

What were the consequences to you?
- What was the impact on you? What did it cost you? Substantively? Emotionally?
- What behavior did it provoke?
- Clarify whether the impact was a consequence of a correct reading of the intention behind the other's behavior or was it a distortion.

- The objective is that the other person acknowledges understanding what you have communicated.

What is the other person's feedback to you?
- Request the other party to give you feedback the same way.
- The objective is for you to acknowledge that you understand the other person.

How do we re-contract to go forward in the relationship?
- Describe your boundary conditions.
- What will you accept and not accept in the future? Pose the same questions for the other person.
- The objective is shared understanding and shared awareness.

The ground rules for strategic dialogue and relational dialogue are tools to overcome the common limiting factor in effective organizational transformation: the impairment of effective dialogue. "To change the behavior of the system, you must identify and change the limiting factor," as Senge states. The minimum, in our experience, is helping the clients engage in strategic dialogue. Facilitating strategic dialogue is not always enough and facilitating relational dialogue may also be necessary in order to build trust. Trust is the lubricant for effective strategic dialogue.

Examples of strategic and relational dialogue from Genesis cases (Section 2)

The comprehensive four year process of organizational transformation and development, facilitated by Arri, engaged multiple levels of the organization in both strategic and relational dialogue, beginning with the leadership team. (See Long-term Improvement, Chapter 11) The process began as a merger integration between Bluefields and Greenfields (fictitious names) and evolved into a continuous transformation process of organizational development and improvement. Over the four years, the transformation process progressed consistently and effectively through the tenures of two CEOs. Each CEO, in turn, led the transformation process by employing the Genesis methodology: mobilizing commitment to craft and implement the operating framework for the business. What evolved was an increasing engagement of the top management teams in constructively learning how to adapt their behaviors by employing relational dialogue to strengthen their trust in one another. They simultaneously implemented the operating framework. And each year they delivered the targeted business results.

Some meetings were entirely focused on relationships and entailed the giving and receiving of feedback to optimize learning and strengthen and/or repair relationships. At the other times, the meetings were primarily strategic and addressed the design and implementation of the newly merged company. As the story unfolded over the years, Arri wove together a sequence of meetings that balanced relational dialogue, conflict resolution and strategic dialogue. To support the clients in their learning to become more effective in dialogue he provided them with experiences outside the realm of business to help them discover the important role that emotions play in decision making and building trust. These included singing and martial arts that were guided by instructors with whom Arri has worked closely and who tailored their work to fit with the overall meeting designs. In debriefing the experiences with the clients, Arri guided their gaining awareness of the connection of their own emotions to their own behavior and the unintended consequences that their behavior sometimes has. The result was that the clients became mobilized to become more effective in how they behaved with their colleagues.

The first CEO, "Leonard", had been receiving more and more questions about the next steps in the recently announced merger. Arri's interviews confirmed that people across the entire organization were concerned about several issues: their personal futures, when decisions would be taken and what the new organization would look like. Leonard and Arri decided to address these questions and anxieties directly, in order to engage the resistance directly. Leonard convened the first Leadership Conference with the top four levels of the Greenfields organization.

The purpose of the Leadership Conference was three-fold: first, to reinforce the business targets for the coming year (Year 2) and the necessity to achieve them; secondly, to validate the output from the interviews Arri had conducted at the outset of the project to diagnose the organization's needs and to further identify any other organizational barriers to performance; thirdly, to inform the people on the planned key steps to integrate the merger with Bluefields. Approximately 150 managers of Greenfields were invited. The top levels of management of the newly acquired Bluefields organization were later invited to a separate conference with the same objectives.

Leonard opened the conference with an overview. As input for the section of the conference regarding organization, Arri presented a synthesis of the interviews, including the concerns and anxieties. Next, sub-groups were given time to validate and/or amend the interview findings and report their conclusions back to the full plenary. Awareness was shared by all that the change would not be easy and individuals were anxious. They addressed issues of both strategy and relationships. A set of recommendations resulted which proved essential in designing the next steps of the organizational change process. They addressed the broad areas of focus that Leonard wanted his organization to achieve during this moment of turbulent, complex change.

The day concluded with a one hour presentation from Leonard in which he summarized highlights from the day, the macro steps and timing of the merger process going forward and the key steps of the process of appointments to the new organization. By then all knew by when their uncertainty and anxiety would be alleviated and their key questions would be answered: "Do I have a job? If so, what is it?" Leonard also announced that no later than the beginning of December, a few months later, he would appoint the members of his new senior management team.

Leonard emphasized that delivering results was dependent upon:
Clarity in the market—not disturbing relationships with customers and consumers
Clarity for the people (everyone within the company)—giving them security and self-confidence
Clarity of Leadership—in direction and decision making

This meeting was an early step in building shared awareness that everyone would be engaged in the change process and that would ultimately result later, in the formulation of the operating framework of the new Greenfields organization. The meeting also was a turning point in improving the relative level of comfort of the people with the merger.

Being informed and having been able to give input began to ameliorate the anxiety of the unknown consequences of the merger. Most everyone felt heard and involved in the change process. The shared awareness resulted in positive energy across the entire group. The culture of dialogue had been introduced.

The meeting was also a platform for Leonard to communicate and further consolidate his leadership. Through the meeting design, his words and his choice of consultant, everyone became aware that he encouraged feedback and listening and was committed to continue to involve a wide and diverse number of people from both companies across multiple geographies and functions. He also provided clear direction on the transformation processes that would unfold; and he unambiguously reinforced the importance of focusing on and delivering business results.

As the transformation process unfolded, Leonard resigned as CEO for personal reasons and was replaced by "Julio". Toward the end of the four year transformation process, Julio and Arri agreed to renew the focus on aligning behaviours to implement agreements. Julio decided to continue developing the Senior Management Team to lead the organization by example. They planned a meeting, grounded in relational dialogue, to be facilitated by Arri. It was aimed at furthering the effectiveness of the relationships between and among the Senior Management Team members so that team members would strengthen their support for one another in realizing their potential as individuals and as a team. They were guided by Arri in the process of giving one another feedback for learning (see above, Ground Rules for Relational Dialogue), once again, culminating in personal commitments from each team member in the form of "I will" statements.

The meeting began with the Senior Management Team assessing its effectiveness as a team, in terms of the criteria established by the parent company. Next the ground rules for feedback and the format to be used for the personal feedback sessions were introduced by Arri. During the majority of time in the meeting, the members gave one another feedback on their respective behaviors. They came to awareness that, as a team, they needed to strengthen their process of understanding the bases for their decisions. Their bias for action, common to many corporate management teams, had led them to a pattern of rapid decision making in meetings, without thorough shared understanding of the reasons behind those decisions. The result, as they saw it, was a pattern of disjointed and incomplete implementation of decisions, frustration and friction among members of the team.

The awareness mobilized their energy to become skilful at strategic dialogue and take the time to develop shared understanding before decisions were taken. They decided in future business meetings to penetrate more rigorously into the analysis of data and to build different, optional scenarios for action as the basis for decision making. They also became aware that improving their team problem solving ability would be facilitated by continuing to strengthen their relationships. With improved trust, their dialogue on ideas would improve as they heard each other more deeply and became more curious about what each other thought. As the case reveals further, over the years, the organization's business results improved and not surprisingly, so did morale.

Lessons in strategic and relational dialogue

Business results are enhanced by both effective strategic and relational dialogue.

If execution of decisions is problematic and/or important relationships between managers are strained, relational dialogue to strengthen trust and mutual understanding is a necessary condition to enable effective strategic dialogue.

Both strategic and relational dialogue can be enhanced by the self awareness of the parties to the dialogue, through each of their own processes of inner dialogue. As the individual becomes more aware of personal emotional drivers to behavior and how personal behavior has produced intended and unintended impacts, the individual can be more effective in relational dialogue and in strategic dialogue.

Chapter 3
Goal: Mobilizing Commitment

One of our multinational clients has been employing our services over a period of more than seventeen years. We have supported them in their ongoing process of adapting their organization and culture to the competitive demands and opportunities of the global economy. They have told us frequently that they have chosen to work with us and our participative, dialogue-centered approach in order to mobilize commitment across their organizations for implementation.

The work with them has comprised two phases. The first phase was the creation of regional divisions around the world through the integration of previously, semi-autonomous country organizations. This included a period of approximately four years when Arri and I teamed up to work in sequence with three European Divisions and the Latin American Division. The pinnacle of this period was the work with the Latin American Division. The CEO shared our philosophy of widespread participation in designing and implementing the new organization. The enthusiasm of the managers echoed across the entire multinational organization. After a few years, this division's performance began to exceed planned expectations year after year. Their process of transformation and the resultant organization design became known as the gold standard for regionalization. Other divisions decided to follow suit. Over another period of approximately three years Michael and I teamed up to work with the Middle East/ North Africa Division and the (rest of) Africa Division to support them in regionalizing, as well.

The second phase of working with this multinational has focused on the support for new global divisions, particularly marketing divisions, in their interface with regional divisions to assure that global strategies and plans would be implemented. Michael has been doing this work over a period of seven years. One example of that work is Chapter 12, Globalization.

Looking back on the experience, the period of working with the multinational to create regional divisions around the world, which Arri and I facilitated, felt like I was riding a wave. The client had momentum and fortunately our approach fit their needs. The work was intense and exciting and led to mobilized commitment and implementation of new organizations with each new project. I see now that the success also had costs.

In those days, Arri and I restricted our work to strategic dialogue. We did not did not engage the clients in relational dialogue explicitly to strengthen trusting relationships in their leadership teams. I had not yet developed the awareness of the importance of blending explicit trust building and relational dialogue with strategic dialogue to achieve results. Trusting relationships did develop, nonetheless, yet only as an implicit by-product of the strategic work. My hunch is the trust developed as a function of the shared strategic successes the leadership teams had in reaching agreements and implementing them.

The focus on strategic dialogue was reinforced by the consistent positive feedback we received from the clients. Until they started working with us, they hadn't known how to integrate their many semi-autonomous country organizations into regional entities. Their urgency was high since their country-centric structure was costly and increasingly uncompetitive. Before working with us they had tried incremental approaches and large scale change by fiat. Both approaches had failed. Their culture had not become skilled in the practice of participative strategic dialogue. In working with us on a series of these large scale change efforts, their culture began to absorb strategic dialogue as a means to mobilize commitment across multiple levels and geographies of their global organization.

With all of this intense experience over a number of years I felt my skills at facilitating strategic dialogue getting sharper. As a corollary, I tended to ignore signs in the clients' systems that relationship problems could be a barrier to mobilizing commitment to implementation. In one of our projects, the CEO did not constructively confront some of his direct reports whose behavior bordered on the insubordinate. These managers had followed a semi-independent path toward implementation. While I observed the behavior, I did not support the CEO in dealing with the relationship problems. Overall, I thought that the change process was moving in the right direction; these problems did not impede the overall process. As I write these words, they sound more like a rationalization than an accurate analysis. The organization spanned all of Europe and had 20,000 employees and these problems seemed to me not to have been too much of a block to implementation. I was busy with one meeting after another making apparent progress on the integration. The CEO dealt with the resistance through organizational politics. He employed help from his superiors, when possible; and he made deals with the resistors by giving them added responsibility which meant added prestige, power and money.

I now see I could have intervened. The implementation could have been smoother and more robust if I had supported the CEO and the direct reports who opposed him to have worked through their differences openly. I also now believe that another barrier which stood in my way was my own lack of self awareness, a function of my not entering into my own inner dialogue. In retrospect I can remember my own discomfort and confusion as to how I might have supported the CEO in addressing his relationship problems. Instead of confronting my discomfort and confusion, I suppressed those feelings.

Mobilizing commitment

To mobilize commitment means to convert potential energy into kinetic energy within the individual, the team and the entire organization. It also means that individuals apply their energy through actions that are aligned with the objectives of the team and/or organization.

Effective leaders mobilize commitment across the entire organization over the course of the macro process. They do this by consulting with multiple internal and external stakeholders, beginning with their own leadership team and next level managers. In so doing they convene meetings in which both strategic and relational dialogue are employed. They facilitate shared awareness at critical moments in those meetings.

The catalyst for mobilized commitment on the macro level of the organization is shared awareness among team members during discussions of what needs to be done and why. Improved performance and organizational results over time are the consequence of mobilized commitment.

Leaders frequently find it difficult to mobilize commitment for change and find themselves pushing, persuading, cajoling, rewarding, punishing and failing. The leaders of our multinational client had had lots of experience with this negative cycle before asking for our assistance. They were ready to try a new approach, one grounded in widespread participation across their organization. As they came to learn through our work together, dialogue and shared awareness between people with previously differing or even conflicting views can happen. The result is mobilized commitment and implementation of the desired organizational change.

Mobilizing Commitment

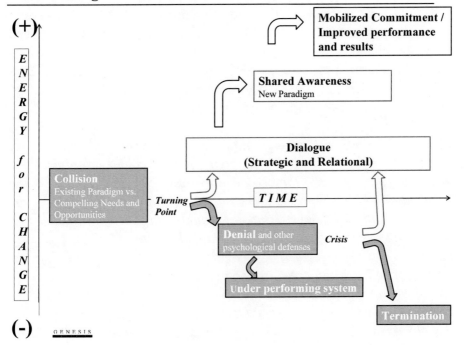

Mobilizing commitment is catalyzed by the *collision* between the *compelling needs and opportunities* on the one side and the *existing paradigm* on the other. This may apply to the organization, the team or the individuals in a relationship. The compelling needs and opportunities are found in the organization's external and internal environments. The existing paradigm of an organization represents its modus operandi and comprises shared mental models of what the business model is and should be as well as shared emotional habits and behaviors which define the culture.

The environment is continually dynamic and in collision with the existing paradigm of the organization. With multinationals, for instance, the global economy continually generates new compelling needs, as adroit competitors compete with their innovative business models, products, brands and new technologies at ever lower costs. The multinationals also continuously discover compelling opportunities in new markets or discover new products in existing markets.

As the *compelling needs and opportunities* collide with the *existing paradigm*, a *turning point* is reached. With one path people in the system inadvertently find refuge in *denial*. They are not yet aware of the need to change the existing paradigm of the way business has and is being done. Results tend to falter as performance the old way becomes less effective. Leaders and members throughout the organization continue to feel increasing pressure to reverse the slide.

This was the case with our multinational client, described at the outset of this chapter. After decades of relying on the country organizations to deliver their results, they could not strengthen their results to the satisfaction of their shareholders or their senior management. Some leaders began to recognize that the country organization model had become an expensive liability. They wanted to make changes and were uncertain how to proceed. They recognized that the country model served as a block in leveraging resources and know-how. As a corporation they couldn't respond to fast and effective global moves by multinational competitors who were more advanced in their global organization designs. Leaders with this view were initially considered "radical" and were met by denial of the problems and defense of the traditional country organizational model. The community of leaders in this corporation had arrived at a stressful turning point.

As we began working with each of the divisions of the multinational through initial meetings with the leadership teams, stress and associated friction in relationships were common. Each division's CEO who invited us to work with him saw the need and opportunity to integrate the country organizations into one regional organization. Yet, in each division some of the country managers predictably argued to defend the autonomy of the country organization. They resisted the loss of control of certain local country functions to the regional organization, particularly manufacturing, R&D and marketing strategy. Yet each of our client divisional CEOs, within the multinational, was eager to implement the regional organization and achieve its promise of efficiencies, economies of scale, growth and profitability.

Through our work with the first of the series of divisions to regionalize, a new organizational paradigm emerged. Instead of the country organization being the "pillar" of the multinational, the country organization became one of four pillars. The other three were the regional leadership team, the regional marketing organizations known as categories and the regional functions such as R&D and Manufacturing. Arri and I, as consultants, formulated this new paradigm. In Gestalt terms, it represented a new figure. The leaders heartily embraced the new framework. A new awareness of how to organize had taken hold. The new paradigm supported the benefits of creating the regional organization; it permitted leveraging the resources of the multinational more effectively across the entire region. The succeeding divisions that enlisted us to help them regionalize readily emulated the breakthrough established by the first division. As we recently learned from one of our client leaders at the time, the awareness had begun to mobilize commitment across the entire multinational and was employed through successive iterations of modifying the global organization.

The turning point between choosing to mobilize commitment or not is also characterized by inevitable differences among managers. Innovative managers are quick to see and acknowledge the collision between the compelling needs and opportunities of the environment and the modus operandi of the organization. Others avoid or deny the new reality and remain defenders of the status quo. The two camps can become polarized and antagonistic.

In one of our regional integration projects, the CEO found that his boss, the chairman of the corporation, was not ready to approve the closing of redundant and costly factories. The chairman was concerned that the resultant layoffs would represent a political problem with unions and potentially with national governments as well. The CEO felt that those problems could be managed through diplomacy. The disagreement escalated. The CEO won the battle in the short term, yet ultimately was forced to resign. The relationship between the CEO and the chairman had become irreparably harmed by the confrontation. The CEO had embraced the process of dialogue within his division in working with us as consultants while at the same time he had been unable to engage his boss in a comparable process. As consultants, we could not intervene in the conflict between the CEO and his chairman, boss, since the CEO had been our client and the chairman had not been.

As the team engages in dialogue, often with guided facilitation, it experiences the virtuous circle of increased self confidence, shared awareness and mobilized commitment. It reconstructs the old organizational paradigm, such as the leadership team did in shifting from the country organization as the pillar of their organization design to the four pillar model. New mental models are assimilated; new emotional habits are learned; new behaviors take hold; and the culture, business model, structure and processes are changed constructively. The leader engages the organization in ever wider rings of dialogue, from the senior management team to the front line. Commitment continues to be mobilized.

The process of working with the multinational to help them regionalize a series of divisions around the world sequentially stretched over a period of more than seven years. In the later years, we found an increasing recognition among managers that their organizations had been underperforming. With that awareness, they were ready to roll up their sleeves, learn from the colleagues who had already regionalized and redesign their organizations with collaborative processes for strengthened performance. Organizational learning had taken hold. Awareness across organizational boundaries had mobilized commitment for change.

Other leaders, faced with comparable challenges at the turning point when the environment begins to collide with the modus operandi, are afflicted with defensiveness and respond with dysfunctional behaviors that exacerbate the current problems. They may deny and be blind to the problems. Or they may see the problems and attempt to cover them up; work harder with existing strategies to resolve them; or displace responsibility onto others. They may also be the victims of groupthink, such as the closed thinking manifested by true believers, "a condition where one only listens to those who are already in lock step agreement, reinforcing set beliefs and creating a situation ripe for miscalculation, also known as incestuous amplification," as described in a US military publication. One potential outcome is the chronic underperforming organization.

The state of denial generates a vicious cycle whereby compelling needs and opportunities from the market and associated pressures and demands from stakeholders continually increase while results continue to falter. Stress increases. This pattern results in another turning point—*the crisis*. The confrontation between the CEO and the chairman, above, was such a crisis.

The leader and organization may emerge from defensiveness and crisis with the shock that the problems are no longer deniable and they finally "see the light". The pressure has built too long. They finally begin to engage others in dialogue openly to diagnose the situation, plan and take appropriate action.

The other path which resolves the crisis is *termination*. This was the fate of the CEO after the crisis with his boss, the chairman. When the leader and the organization remain stuck in denial and resistance, trusting relationships with stakeholders are eroded. Termination can take various forms: leaders may get fired or resign, the business may go bankrupt and the organization may be dissolved or acquired. As we saw in the multinational over the years, a few country managers could not support the regionalization of their divisions and remained stuck in defensiveness. They either were fired or voluntarily left the organization.

The model, Mobilizing Commitment, had its roots in my doctoral dissertation, ICAR, Illusion, Crisis, Awareness, Realignment (1980). I wrote about a consulting assignment I had had with a New York City high school aimed at improving the school by developing involvement of students, parents, teachers, administrators and other stakeholders. With all the enthusiasm of a neophyte I hoped that not only would I have material for a dissertation, I would also have a story about a consulting success.

I began writing the dissertation while the project was unfolding. In a fateful meeting with the client, the principal, I learned that she was disappointed with our progress and I had missed several problems. I feared that I would be fired. I was dismayed. I consulted my thesis advisor, Chris Argyris. It was he who suggested that the thesis could be an analysis of the failure. I took a deep breath and proceeded to try and understand what I had done wrong. As he suggested, my "compulsion for success" had blinded me to the problems in the project. I became aware that the early phase of the project had been my illusion-phase. The meeting with the principal represented the crisis. Either I would be fired or I would be able to proceed and try to rectify the problems. With the client's willingness, we continued to engage in dialogue and proceeded to work together. We reviewed what the problems had been and how we had missed them. This was the phase of awareness. Finally, we instituted changes in our approach which represented the phase of realignment. In retrospect, and applying the lenses of the model, Mobilizing Commitment, the principal and I had entered into dialogue at the beginning of the crisis and continued in dialogue through the awareness and realignment phases.

In the literature review for the dissertation I discovered that my process had been by no means unique. Thomas Kuhn, the eminent philosopher of science, in his classic book, <u>The Structure of Scientific Revolutions</u>, described that the evolution of scientific thought has followed a similar process. Also around that time I saw an Ingmar Bergman movie, "Scenes of a Marriage"; a story of marriage, betrayal, separation, divorce and reconciliation. Upon reading Kuhn and seeing the movie I crystallized my model as having the phases of illusion, crisis, awareness and realignment.

Kuhn examined the history of science and described how repeatedly an existing paradigm would be eventually disconfirmed by the accumulation of new scientific data. This is the process which I have come to describe as the collision of compelling needs and opportunities with the existing paradigm of the organization. Initially the disconfirming data would be rejected by society. Finally, the disconfirming data would be explained by an innovator with a new paradigm that would ultimately win acceptance. Kuhn used the Copernican revolution as an illustration. Before Copernicus and Galileo, religious doctrine prevailed and the earth was seen as the center of the universe. In their time, the 16th and 17th centuries, they and other astronomers were having increasing difficulty explaining their data to fit the religious belief. Finally, Copernicus and then Galileo asserted that the sun was the center of the universe and demonstrated that the data supported the new paradigm convincingly. The resistance by the Catholic Church and society to the new paradigm was virulent. Galileo was committed to house arrest in 1633 after an ecclesiastical trial. Pope John Paul II and The Pontifical Academy of Sciences exonerated Galileo only in 1992. Some old paradigms die hard.

As my years of consulting experience unfolded I continued to evolve the ICAR model into what has now become the model of Mobilizing Commitment. I discovered that the heart of the ICAR process had been dialogue.

In retrospect, it was through dialogue with my client and my thesis advisor that I was able to move through the crisis of apparent failure and become aware of what happened and what could be done to improve the situation. The concept of awareness was fundamental to ICAR and as I was later to learn, fundamental to Gestalt therapy, as well. As Gestalt scholars describe (e.g. Nevis and Melnick), awareness catalyzes constructive energy. This was certainly true for me. Through awareness I was able to learn from my illusion that all had been going well and understand my mistakes. Learning to be aware of a situation with a client not going well helped me to become more helpful to my client at the time and to become more helpful to future clients, as well. The awareness also unleashed the energy in me to complete my dissertation.

Examples of mobilizing commitment from Genesis cases (Section 2)

Accelerated Strategy Development, the Chapter 13 case, was facilitated by Kees. His client, the CEO of HMM, was clear at the outset. He wanted a strategy for aggressively expanding his company's penetration of the China market; he wanted a quality strategy; and he wanted a strategy with a high probability that it would be successfully implemented. He intended to mobilize the commitment of key managers to develop and implement the strategy. He also wanted to transform a culture he felt was too cautious and slow to act. Based on his prior work with Kees, he chose the participative dialogue-centered process he knew that Kees would deliver.

The CEO, while leading another company a few years earlier, had experienced success with Kees who facilitated an intensive, cross-functional meeting method designed to solve complex problems rapidly. Based on GE's famous Workout! Methodology, the "30-60-90 Day Process", as the CEO named it, focused on implementation of plans within 90 days of an intensive three day planning meeting. Rigorous progress reviews were held at the 30 day and 60 day milestones.

Recognizing the importance of involving all key stakeholders across geographies and functions, the CEO invited his peer, the CEO of another subsidiary of the parent company, also in China, to join him as co-sponsor. The two subsidiaries needed to collaborate since they shared some customers and both needed to work with regional and national governmental entities.

The CEO challenged his team with a goal that he believed was feasible and deliberately ambitious to shake up their culture of caution: $500 million in sales in China in five years, over three times the current sales volume and achievement of parity with the HMM, Inc.USA business, historically, the largest regional business within HHM. He also challenged the new China region to become the primary source for components and sub-assemblies for HHM's world-wide operations. And he wanted the strategy meeting to occur within a few months. These goals were huge and unheard of for HHM. In aggregate, they represented a long term commitment to China far beyond the next five years and a dramatic change of culture from caution to calculated risk.

The CEO was considered a daring leader by his subordinates. He staked much on a single 3 day meeting and the 90 day process to follow. He risked his own reputation by putting himself on the line publicly with his superior and his subordinates. He also put constructive pressure on the facilitator, Kees and all the cross-functional participants who were to be invited to the meeting, as well as his full management team. He believed in all of them that they would succeed.

The CEO and Kees assured that all the necessary expertise and managerial roles required for the strategy were represented by the participants. The meeting was designed by Kees so that the participants engaged in intensive, creative, strategic dialogue. Relational dialogue was not considered as a complement, since the strategic dialogue methodology, by itself, had proven itself effective over the years for solving discrete business challenges. The preparations had been rigorous; all participants had done their homework. The strategic dialogue was rich and at the conclusion, the participants were happy, proud and motivated. They had achieved more than they expected—the first draft of a strategy which they all understood and owned. The CEO had succeeded in mobilizing commitment to the new strategy.

Lessons in mobilizing commitment

Leading transformation of an organization to strengthen results requires mobilizing commitment across the entire organization.

Mobilizing commitment can take time, beginning with the senior team and expanding to ever wider concentric rings of managers and employees through dialogue and the resultant shared awareness.

Denial, resistance and conflict inevitably are part of the transformation process. By employing dialogue, the client system can overcome these barriers and strengthen trust. As dialogue becomes more practiced and trust strengthens, a virtuous cycle is catalyzed. The capacity of the client system to engage effectively in further dialogue and mobilize commitment for transformation improves.

Chapter 4
Barriers: Different Perceptions, Different Realities

Three departmental managers and their CEO were stuck in acrimonious debates regarding budget allocations and investments in potential new businesses. I was contracted to mediate their dispute. Each of the managers felt that historically the other managers repeatedly had acted unfairly to advance the fortunes of their own departments. When they and the CEO called me, they had reached yet another impasse and recognized that they couldn't find an effective way to negotiate with one another. The three managers had had deep friction among themselves throughout their careers in the same company. They each had a different version of their shared history. Each had a list of "wrongs" perpetrated by their colleagues to their own personal disadvantage. They were long term members of a highly internal competitive corporate culture and two were fighters and one was more withdrawn. The CEO's attitude was that the three of them should "sort it out".

As the mediation proceeded and the managers achieved some interim agreements, they began to experience that they could actually collaborate. Nonetheless, they continued to refer to the past "misdeeds" of their colleagues. It was only minimally that they acknowledged the agreements which they had recently made. Each one, in their own way, expressed cognitive dissonance: yes, agreements have been made and there has been progress in the mediation and collaboration, yet, at the same time "I cannot trust my colleagues to behave any differently than I have known them since the beginning."

I found each manager actually began to strive for a fair budget allocation process. Nonetheless, each of the managers repeatedly characterized the behavior of the others in negative terms with attributions such as "he/she is trying to hijack the process or sabotage the process or twist the process for personal gain." After working with the team for over one and one half years, the managers had made progress on some interim agreements, yet their trust in one another failed to significantly improve.

The terms of my contract focused on helping them resolve the substantive disagreements among the three managers. During the contracting two of the three resolutely had ruled out explicitly working on building trust and did not want to engage in any activities akin to team building. With some hesitation, I accepted the terms. It seemed feasible to help them find agreements since the problems presented were substantive and centered on resource allocation. I was not yet aware of how deeply rooted and long lasting the lack of trust among the three managers had been.

Now I have seen that the system of the three managers has become only marginally more effective in spite of achieving a series of interim agreements. Trust has strengthened between two of the three managers. Yet a polarity has emerged; those two vs. the other one. Repeatedly I have pointed out that one source of their chronic conflict is that perception is reality and the perceptions and realities of the three of them have consistently differed. Only one of the three, the more withdrawn manager, could acknowledge this phenomenon.

As of this writing the process continues. I have been challenged by attempting to support these chronically conflicted people to reach agreement; frustrated by the slow pace and continuous suspicion the parties have had of one another; pleased that they did achieve some significant interim agreements; and fascinated by the complexity of this dilemma. On multiple occasions I have felt that the individual managers have taken positions less for reasons of substantive personal benefit and more out of a residue of resentment and anger at their colleagues. When I have fed back these observations to the individuals in question, I have typically been met with denial.

This was a case in which the clients were committed to the strategic dialogue of the mediation only, and shunned any effort on my part to engage in relational dialogue with one another. This case has proved to be another example of the common phenomenon that perceptions of the other party in conflict are difficult to unfreeze.

Different perceptions, different realities

We perceive our reality with mental and emotional tools to help us decide, consciously and unconsciously, how to respond to that reality. These tools are perceptual and serve as filters so we can attend to what we consider, a priori, to be important while we can ignore the rest. As psychological and neurological research continues to develop, we are now learning the brain's emotional filters reside in the limbic system which lurks beneath consciousness. Emotional filters are learned and become emotional habits. A graphic example is an individual who suffers from post traumatic stress disorder (PTSD). This individual will feel a spike in anxiety by any cue that is even unconsciously reminiscent of the trauma. A soldier with PSTD who is back home may have an anxiety attack simply, for example, by hearing a car back fire that is reminiscent of the explosion he witnessed which took the life of a companion.

Our cognitive filters reside in the frontal cortex and are the mental models or paradigms which help us understand events and how to respond to them. In war, cognitive filters contribute to the process of demonizing the enemy.

The filters of emotional habits and mental models embody our implicit assumptions, belief systems, values, biases, prejudices, rivalries and loyalties. Consequently, different perceptions of the same situation by different people may result in different realities.

Facilitators of organizational transformation facilitate moments of shared awareness, meetings of dialogue and macro processes over time to mobilize commitment. The result is that the teams who participate tend to resolve their differing perceptions, agree on facts, build trust and ultimately share their reality.

Perception derives from one's mental models and emotional habits, as well as from one's formal position in the organization. Mental models refer to the values and beliefs that are the cognitive constructs one uses consciously and unconsciously to make sense of reality. Mental models shape what one sees and doesn't see, as well as what one understands and doesn't understand. While the cliché says I'll believe it if I see it, perceptual psychologists and philosophers such as Kuhn have demonstrated that it is more accurate to say, "I'll only see it if I believe it".

Many of our client organizations have exemplified the power of mental models as central to the common dynamic of resistance to change. The multinational described above had a culture where the powerful mental model of the country organization was deeply maintained, even in the face of considerable evidence that it was a structure that no longer served the corporation well in the global market. The various management teams discovered that the proposed change—toward regional and global structures—clashed with the existing mental models that the resistors clung to of how the organization had been and should continue to be.

The companion filter to mental models is the set of one's emotional habits. These are the internalized emotional reactions we experience when triggered by certain, specific circumstances. They are learned, mostly unconsciously, throughout our lives, from our families, our life experiences and the culture around us. Neurological researchers have identified structures in the brain, especially the limbic system, where emotional memories reside outside of conscious awareness. This research also has revolutionized our understanding of decision making. Emotions are integral; there is no such thing as a purely rational decision. Emotional self awareness is essential for leaders as they seek to continue to build trusting relationships and make decisions which mobilize commitment across the organization.

A client CEO was leading a discussion with his team on a potential strategic direction which he thought was important for the organization. This was the first time he had discussed it with his team. The CEO solicited feedback from the team. Questions of clarification, doubts with regard to efficacy and explicit criticisms emerged. The CEO began to show tension in his facial expressions. He began to counter the criticisms and rapidly answer the questions. The team members pushed a little longer and then withdrew and became silent. He somewhat defiantly closed the discussion with the statement that he appreciated the input and he still intended to move forward on the strategic option. As I had been serving as an observer in order to provide feedback to the CEO after the meeting, later, I asked the CEO how he had felt during the discussion. He acknowledged that he had felt irritation with several members of the team. He attributed self-serving motives to their questions and challenges. I probed deeper. He began to admit that he had felt embarrassed and not well prepared. With that awareness he began to explore how he might have handled the discussion with greater openness. He also decided to re-open the discussion with this team and retract his premature decision to go forward.

Emotional habits strongly influence our relationships with others. This has been true with the managers described above, at the introduction to this chapter. They continue to manifest the emotional habits of low trust and conflict, even in the face of experiences where collaboration has begun to emerge.

Psychotherapy, including some forms of executive coaching, supports the client in discovering emotional habits and how they may have distorted current perceptions and led to counterproductive behavior. The combination of mental models and emotional habits contributes to vast differences in perceived realities. In the international organizations with whom we work there are multiple cultural differences. Managers frequently come from different nationalities with different native languages; they also represent different functions in the organization and are stationed in different geographies. They also have different stakes in whatever transformation is being planned. In our example of the multinational that was creating integrated regional structures, initially those with a stake in creating the regional organization, such as the CEO, had different perceptions than the country managers, who initially saw their stake as maintaining their country organizations. The CEO perceived all the benefits and the country managers saw all the risks with proceeding. Through dialogue, they were able to understand each other's perceptions and arrived at a shared awareness. Ultimately, they were able to implement the new integrated regional organization together.

Example of Different perceptions, different realities from the cases to follow (Section 2)

The phenomenon that perception is reality and differing perceptions can be a barrier to trust had been a factor during the years of Michael's process of facilitating the integration of the Division I Purchasing Organization from being regional units to becoming one, integrated global unit (see Chapter 12).

It became even more of a challenge in the fifth year when senior management decided to integrate the Division I and Division II purchasing organizations globally. Resistance to the merger was high. The managers of each division had harbored negative perceptions of the other. Further, the managers feared that their jobs were at risk. The purchasing roles in Division I and Division II were duplicative in each region around the world and the merger would result in the creation of one purchasing leadership team in each region and the elimination of the duplicate jobs. There was also a belief shared by some managers in both divisions that the business models of the two divisions were incompatible. Division I was believed to be well suited to global purchasing given its many global brands. Whereas Division II was believed to require local and regional purchasing since their products and brands translated less well globally and required local and regional modifications to suit consumer needs.

The global SVPs of Manufacturing of the two divisions had appointed Ludwig as the manager to lead the merger integration of the Division I and Division II purchasing organizations, just as he led the integration of the Division I regions into one global organization. Ludwig once again invited Michael to continue to facilitate the process with him. The two convened a kick-off meeting with the lead purchasing managers of Division I and Division II. In agreement with the two SVPs, Ludwig and Michael, aware of the antagonistic differing perceptions of the managers of the two divisions toward one another, established the objectives for the meeting as follows:

- Establish a common basis of understanding of how we each operate in our respective Divisions.
- Identify some concrete opportunities to unlock value through joint management of materials used by both Divisions and agree on an implementation plan to realize them.

- Identify common gaps in purchasing capabilities and develop a shared agenda to address them.
- Agree (or agree to disagree) on some fundamental organizing principles for One MNX Purchasing across the two Divisions.

The feelings of the managers in both Divisions were conflicted going into the meeting. While they were resistant, they also understood and accepted the expectations of their superiors that they could and must deliver significant cost savings, efficiencies and bottom line benefits for MNX through an integration of the two Divisions' Purchasing Units.

Once again, the preparation for the meeting began with a round of interviews by Michael. The reasons for their resistance were reiterated by many. Further, the Division II Global Purchasing Leadership Team members also reported negative perceptions of Ludwig, whom they did not yet know except by reputation, and considered his proactive style as over-controlling or worse. Given the close and trusting relationship between Michael and Ludwig, Michael advised Ludwig to play a low-key role in the upcoming meeting—"don't be directive; don't lecture; let me facilitate the process". Ludwig heeded the advice. Michael presented the interview synthesis at the outset of the meeting. It served as a mirror to all the participants; they saw their lack of mutual understanding and negative history forthrightly. They could now address them as barriers to overcome.

The interviews also served as the data from which Michael had facilitated the negotiations to agree on the objectives for the meeting between and among Ludwig, and the SVPs of Manufacturing of the two Divisions.

The first phase of the meeting was designed to address the resistant perceptions from both sides. The Division I team saw Division II as unjustifiably arrogant; the Division I team also saw themselves as having had much more experience with global purchasing. The Division II team saw Division I as threatening; they feared that they would be "taken over" by Division I. Division II managers recognized that the Division I Global Purchasing Leadership Team had already spent four plus years building themselves as an effective team while they, the Division II Global Purchasing Leadership Team, were still a group of individuals working solely in their separate regions.

The first activity of the meeting was designed so that members of the two Divisions could understand each other's perceptions of one another. Pairs were invited to have lunch together, one from each Global Purchasing Leadership Team. The aim was to begin to get to know one another informally and begin to establish trust. Upon return from the lunch each individual reported on what they learned about each other. This discussion progressed into a discussion of a shared vision of what the attributes of a unified Purchasing organization for MNX could be in five years.

Next, the two Global Purchasing Leadership Teams were invited to meet separately and engage in a humorous exercise that would prove to be insightful. Each group was asked to illustrate three groups with an animal as a metaphor:
Yourselves, your own Global Purchasing Leadership Team
Your counterparts, the other Global Purchasing Leadership Team
Together, the intended integrated Global Purchasing Leadership Team
The result was laughter and the further building of personal connections and trust between the two groups. The awareness was clear, the Division I and II managers had different and negative perceptions of one another. Until they communicated them to one another, those perceptions had been their realities.

Another exercise was employed to help the members of the two Global Purchasing Leadership Teams overcome their differences. They engaged in martial arts facilitated by a karate black belt who was also a psychologist. The title for the exercise was "buyers as warriors". Through the shadow boxing exercise, the karate psychologist facilitated the debriefing so that the participants could examine the emotions of the inter-group competition that they brought to the meeting. The awareness helped them shift their emotions, in the next phases of the meeting, from hostility to cooperation.

All of these exercises helped the managers from the two Divisions to relinquish their prior negative perceptions of one another as "the other group" and to begin accepting each other as individuals. The process of building trust had begun.

The meeting then proceeded to the substantive work of exploring areas of collaboration and action planning. At the end of the meeting, the two SVPs of Manufacturing joined and received reports from the two teams. The reports included not only the animal metaphors that were received once again with laughter, but there was also an impressive list of the substantive, cost saving ideas for prospective collaboration. The meeting was considered a success, by most everyone, both substantively as well as emotionally, as trusting relationships across the divide of the two teams had begun to develop.

Shortly thereafter, the two SVPs decided formally to integrate the Division I and Division II Purchasing organizations and appointed Ludwig as the head of the new, integrated MNX Purchasing Leadership Team.

Once again, Ludwig invited Michael to facilitate the process going forward and they convened what evolved into a series of four organizing meetings of the new MNX Global Purchasing Leadership Team with responsibility for both divisions. The focus continued to be how to help build the new management team and design how the two organizations would work together. Throughout the meetings the new Team worked step by step on continuing to build their trusting relationships, as well as on designing the details of their new organization and operating framework.

The process of trust building between the two Divisions' Purchasing units was extended beyond the leadership teams. The senior managers of the two Divisions collaborated in planning and delivering a meeting with all of their direct reports that involved them in planning further details of the integration.

Lessons in dealing with barriers: different perceptions, different realities

Individuals have different emotional responses to the same situation based on different perceptions resulting in different views of reality. The common and overly simplistic mantra in corporate circles that "decision making must be fact based" can be a trap. Facts can be difficult to agree on, especially on important issues, where people are emotionally invested. Emotions and beliefs, as well as the structure and functioning of the brain all play a role in how perception is reality for the individual. What you "know" to be a fact, may not be seen as a fact by another.

In the dialogue, it is helpful for team members to express their emotions in addition to the facts and logic they use. This way the team can arrive at a shared view of the facts, coupled with appreciation for the emotions of each member. This contributes to a durable consensus.

In a change process individuals commonly find themselves in conflict with one another. The source of the conflict often is the psychological process whereby different individuals have different perceptions of reality and believe that their view is the "truth". Unless the conflicts are resolved, the organizational transformation and associated improvements in results will likely fail. The client system can learn and employ strategic and relational dialogue so that individuals can resolve their conflicts and shift their positions through increased trust and understanding of one another's positions. This will help the antagonists to arrive at a shared perception of reality, including shared perceptions of the facts, a foundation for consensus agreements.

Chapter 5
Fractals: *Moments* of shared awareness, *Meetings* of dialogue and *Macro processes* that mobilize commitment

"The merger process is now beginning; our acquisition offer has been accepted!" CY, the CEO, proudly exclaimed to me. "I want to get moving quickly on building the new global organization. I've got the membership in mind for my new executive team, including managers from both companies, and I want to have a planning retreat with them within in the next month."

He invited my partner, Arri and me to facilitate the overall process since we had developed a trusting relationship with him on a prior organizational transformation project. We had helped him integrate disparate, federated European companies, into one integrated European wide organization over the course of the prior year. The new acquisition now catapulted his company from encompassing Europe alone to now encompassing operations on all continents around the world.

Together we planned the macro process, a series of meetings, beginning with the new senior executive team and expanding to broader concentric rings of managers. The meetings would be led by the CEO and facilitated by Arri and me. To prepare for the first retreat of the new executive team we carried out a series of diagnostic interviews with the members of the new team plus selected other opinion leaders from both companies. The interviews, once consolidated, would serve as the basis for the first executive team retreat when they would design the framework of the company.

As Arri, CY and I discussed the interview findings we reviewed each component of our diagnostic tool, the Urgent Vision model, comprising the business model, the values and culture, the business processes and the organization design (see Chapter 8, for a full definition). Our intention in feeding the data back to the CY, the CEO, was for him to

Chapter 5—Fractals: *Moments* of shared awareness, *Meetings* of
dialogue and *Macro processes* that mobilize commitment

61

*decide, as the leader, what would be the main points of the agenda at
the different phases, especially in the first rounds of meetings with the
new senior team and their next level direct reports. We believed that the
leader's commitment was essential from the beginning.*

*CY was clear. The most important initial issue from his perspective was
that the cultures of the two merged entities were significantly different.
In essence the acquired company was nimbler and more innovative. CY's
acquiring company was more bureaucratic as well as more consistent and
reliable in delivering results. CY wanted to capitalize on the strengths of
the two cultures and avoid a culture clash that could impede the merger
integration process. He decided that the initial focus of the meeting with
the new executive team would be to agree which values would guide the
business. He hoped and we agreed that by agreeing values at the outset
of the merger integration, the codified values could be used to guide
the behaviors of all managers and hold them accountable for living the
values. The values would be the compass to guide the merger integration
process and the management of the new company. Further, the strengths
of both companies could be retained in the newly merged entity.*

*Since it was a small team, CY only wanted one facilitator for the first
meeting. CY selected me, I think because during those relatively early
years of our Genesis partnership, I was perceived as more senior than
Arri. Since CY was Turkish, he held this meeting in his home country of
Turkey. He treated his new team royally. He was already demonstrating
the values of caring, respect, generosity and hospitality. The meeting
focused on team members getting to know each other as individuals
and the integration of the values of the two prior companies. That
list of values became central to the succeeding meetings with larger
groups of managers as everyone was invited to explore and challenge
what they signified for the future of the new company. Ultimately, the
values became codified and became key standards of performance in
the reward and compensation systems.*

*Through successive iterations, Arri and I facilitated meetings involving
more levels of management, the operating framework for guiding the new
organization was developed in greater detail. In a matter of months, the
new organization, including a new corporate identity, was implemented
with considerable shared awareness, ownership and commitment from*

the top three levels of management, comprising over one hundred managers from around the world. The corporate identity was built on the agreed values. The success of the new company was underscored when, a few years later, the parent company sold it for a significant profit.

My work with CY as the client was a joy. CY's enthusiasm for the merger was infectious and an inspiration to his organization. He had worked hard for many months, much of the time in another country away from his home, in negotiating the acquisition, directly with the company to be acquired. Simultaneously he negotiated with his own management to secure the funds necessary. He was exuberant that he had succeeded.

His focus on values, first and foremost, was a refreshing learning experience for me. In all of the other large scale organizational transformation projects that I had facilitated, values (and culture) had always been one dimension, along with the defining of the business model, the business processes and the structure of the new entity. CY made values the "figure", as Gestalt consultants would call it. In so doing, he heightened the awareness of everyone around him, including ourselves, on how attention to values and behavior could be a successful lever to mobilize commitment for implementation even in a global organization. The development of the full operating framework, including the design of the business model, the business processes and the structure unfolded effectively without our further facilitation as consultants.

Chapter 5—Fractals: *Moments* of shared awareness, *Meetings* of
dialogue and *Macro processes* that mobilize commitment

63

**Fractals: moments of awareness, meetings of dialogue and macro
processes to mobilize commitment**

A common definition of **fractal** is a rough or fragmented geometric
shape that can be split into parts, each of which is (at least
approximately) a reduced-size copy of the whole. In the natural world
there are many examples: rivers, trees and leaves, crystals, ferns,
broccoli, lightening, snowflakes, Nautilus shell.

The term fractal is used here as a metaphor for understanding the
relationship of facilitating *moments* of shared awareness, *meetings*
of dialogue and *macro processes* that mobilize commitment and
that we summarize as $F = m^3$. Organizational transformation occurs
on these three inter-related levels simultaneously. The moments are
nested within meetings and meetings are nested within the macro
process. The macro process comprises the set of meetings over time
that engages ever wider rings of stakeholders in dialogue to design
and implement the new organization.

Shared awareness in moments, dialogue in meetings and mobilizing
commitment across macro processes ideally are consistent and
support one another. Together they enable the organization to get from
its current state of compelling needs and opportunities to its desired
state of new behaviors grounded in new mental models and emotional
habits. The facilitator is continuously aware of the three levels—the
moment, the meeting and the macro process—and facilitates to
support their fractal-like consistency. The client learns to become
aware of the three levels and their consistency through the experience
of and reflection on the process.

Facilitating the Moment, the Meeting and the Macro Process

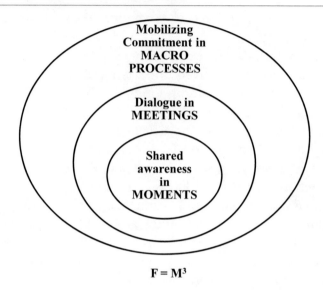

Mobilizing
Commitment in
**MACRO
PROCESSES**

**Dialogue in
MEETINGS**

**Shared
awareness
in
MOMENTS**

$$F = M^3$$

GENESIS

The process of working with CY exemplified the fractal dynamic of facilitating moments of awareness, meetings of dialogue and a macro process to mobilize commitment. The CEO, CY, had asked Arri and me to work with him as facilitators since he was eager to employ dialogue as the means of doing the work of the merger, commencing with the senior team, since he had experienced this way of our working with him and his organization in the past. In our initial planning of the merger integration, he agreed to the macro process whereby we would roll out a series of strategic dialogue oriented meetings with ever wider concentric rings of the newly merged organization. Upon receiving the diagnostic interview data he had the moment of awareness that determined the theme to be addressed in the first round of the macro process: the development of shared values. The series of meetings would begin with the new senior team to be followed by meetings with ever wider concentric rings of next level managers. The successive meetings on the theme of values were well received and filled with positive energy and candor. The macro process unfolded to mobilize commitment across the multiple geographies and

Chapter 5—Fractals: *Moments* of shared awareness, *Meetings* of dialogue and *Macro processes* that mobilize commitment

65

divisions of the global organization. The new company's performance exceeded expectations.

How we facilitate Moments, Meetings and Macro Processes in partnership with our client leaders

All encounters with the client system that we have as facilitators necessarily comprise the three levels simultaneously: the moments are nested in the meetings; and the meetings are nested in the macro process of the series of meetings. We have learned to think and facilitate on these multiple process levels simultaneously: the unfolding moments support the objectives of the meeting and the goals of the macro process.

We are also continuously aware of both the process and the content and help our clients learn that dichotomy. The process refers to the sequence of steps of the macro process that may flow over weeks, months or even years. The process also refers to the design and flow of each meeting and that can emerge spontaneously moment to moment in every meeting, in unexpected directions, as well.

The content refers to the substance of what is being discussed. We become familiar with the substantive business issues that the clients have determined are in need of resolution through the interviews that we conduct before most meetings, and through our ongoing work with the clients. While we are external consultants, we learn to talk the language of our clients and understand the challenges that they face. Yet, as facilitators of the processes we are careful to avoid taking the role of the content expert who gives advice on substantive solutions. Our process facilitation approach is distinct from the expert role that many, if not most, consultants play. They are principally in the business of offering strategic and technical advice to their clients.

The Macro Process to mobilize commitment

In dialogue with the leader-client, the facilitator develops a plan for a series of meetings and coaching sessions designed to address the objectives of the transformation. The design is such that one activity leads naturally and logically to another in a flow. The outcome of one meeting may serve as input to the next.

The meetings of the macro process typically begin with the senior team. These are aimed at defining the framework for the overall change process, as well as strengthening trust in the relationships among the members of the senior team. To do this we employ the Genesis Urgent Vision model (see Chapter 8 for a full definition) and may include any or all of its prime organizational dimensions: strategy and winning business concept, values/behavior/culture, business processes and organizational structure. Strengthening trust in relationships may be addressed with a range of possible activities, from playing games to giving feedback on behavior.

During the early phases of the macro process, the facilitator may also conduct coaching sessions with the CEO and the members of the senior management team. The coaching sessions may be both strategic and relational. Strategic coaching addresses approaches to the unfolding change process, including the roles that the individuals and their departments would play. Relational coaching addresses emotions, behaviors and conflicts that may exist between and among members of the senior team and others in the organization.

Once the senior team has agreed on the framework for the change process, the next series of meetings are typically with the departmental teams of the respective senior team members. These meetings mirror the senior team meeting and are conducted following the principle of "freedom within a framework" (Chapter 6). The departmental teams have the freedom to design their work within that framework. Commonly, the senior team reconvenes for additional meetings to develop more aspects of the new organizational framework. Ultimately, once the senior team feels ready and all departments have participated, then a "Leadership Conference" may be convened that typically involves all managers in the top 3-4 levels of the organization. This large meeting celebrates the implementation of the changes while also involving dialogue centered work, particularly at the interfaces between and among departments. The Leadership Conference symbolically culminates and further supports the process of mobilizing commitment for the transformation of the organization. An example of a Leadership Conference is presented, in detail in Chapter 14, Merger Integration.

Chapter 5—Fractals: *Moments* of shared awareness, *Meetings* of
dialogue and *Macro processes* that mobilize commitment

67

The macro process of mobilizing commitment may also be seen as "concentric rings of dialogue" over time.

A Macro Process of Dialogue to Mobilize Commitment

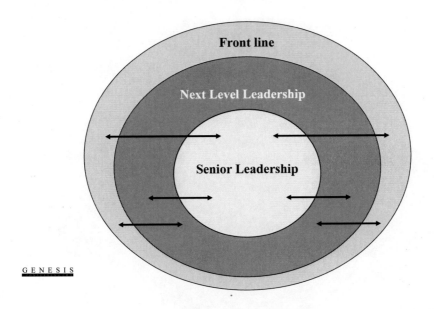

The macro process of mobilizing commitments begins with the senior leadership. Once they have achieved shared understanding through dialogue on the framework for the organization-wide change they engage the next level or two of management in further dialogue and shared understanding. Ultimately the front line is also so engaged. Other key stakeholders are also invited into the process over time, such as customers and suppliers.

Another schematic view of the macro process of mobilizing commitment
puts the spotlight on translating ideas into action.

Macro Process to Mobilize Commitment--
Phases

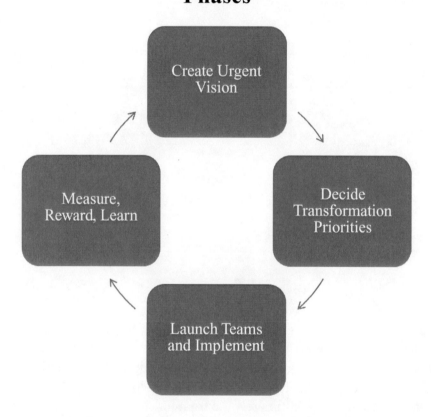

The process of organizational transformation may be seen as beginning
with the creation of the Urgent Vision by the senior team. Within this broad
framework with many potential avenues of action, the senior team settles on
its transformation priorities. These may be directed at changing the culture
and behaviors, the business model and strategies, the business processes
and/or the organization design and structure. To support implementation
and continuous improvement the implementation actions are measured.
Rewards are dispensed for effective implementation and good results. The
process of implementation work is studied to learn how to improve it.
Inherent to this process is dialogue, both relational and strategic.

Chapter 5—Fractals: *Moments* of shared awareness, *Meetings* of
dialogue and *Macro processes* that mobilize commitment

69

The Dialogue Meeting—relational or strategic

Designing the Dialogue Meeting

The facilitator designs the details of each meeting according to the
principles of strategic and/or relational dialogue. Since the sessions
are creative working sessions, we typically call them workshops. The
design of the agenda begins with the leader determining the theme
for the workshop. Next, the facilitator conducts a round of interviews
with all who will participate in the workshop and others who may have
important information to contribute or roles to play which are relevant
to the overall theme. With the input from the interviews, the facilitator
develops the first draft of the agenda, including the exercises to be
employed to assure optimal participation.

The agenda design is finally negotiated with the leader of the team who
also participates in the meeting. The agenda design becomes a contract.
Understanding, ownership and commitment to the agenda by the leader
and the team members are critical factors for success of the meeting
itself. The leader sends out the agenda and support materials in advance
of the meeting to the participants to support their preparation and
symbolically communicate the leader's ownership for and leadership of
the upcoming meeting.

We use the configuration of the room to encourage dialogue and usually
eliminate the table in the middle that can serve as a psychological
barrier between people. Taking away the table is unusual in most
business meetings and communicates that this meeting is about people
connecting with one another.

The meeting design is a flow so one activity and topic leads naturally and
logically to the next one. The outcome of one module within the meeting
frequently serves as input to the next module. The meeting opens with
the leader stating the purpose. Next, in the spirit of dialogue, all members
are invited to share their thoughts and feelings regarding the purpose of
the meeting and the overall macro change process. The facilitator then
presents the ground rules for dialogue, either strategic or relational, as
well as the consultative decision making model. While the leader of
the meeting has already agreed to the ground rules and the decision

making model in the preparation meetings with the facilitator, this is an opportunity for questions and modifications by all participants. The facilitator uses the discussion as a moment of contracting and explains that by agreeing to the ground rules and decision making model, the facilitator will facilitate the meeting accordingly. The agenda explicitly allows that the remainder of the agenda may be modified to reflect any new suggestions.

The interview data are presented at the beginning of each topic in the agenda while highlighting areas of agreement and disagreement. Step by step the meeting unfolds with questions to be answered by the team. The dialogue is facilitated to confirm agreements and resolve disagreements. Confirming agreements helps the team appreciate the progress it is making. Identifying and resolving conflicts takes more time and helps the team come to agreement on significant issues that may be contentious and may have smoldered in the organization for months or even years.

If the team has approximately ten or fewer members, the team usually stays together as one discussion group. Larger groups may be subdivided into smaller working groups who then report back to the whole.

In strategic meetings, we write down the reports from the sub-groups verbatim on the computer that is connected to a projector so the writing is also simultaneously beamed onto a screen. Everyone in the room can see what is reported and an electronic record is kept, as well. Over the years, in Genesis, we have found this technique so helpful that we have developed the keyboard skills to record the highlights of dialogue real time; akin to using a flip chart only in this case it is an "electronic flip chart" and the writing is always legible, more complete and easily fed back quickly to participants.

Utilizing the Consultative Consensus decision making model, the facilitator facilitates consensus where possible and the leader makes the ultimate decision. Reviewing the notes of the discussion that has just occurred is a helpful tool in the decision making process.

In relational meetings, to enhance intimacy and connections between people, we do not use the computer and rarely use flip charts, either.

Chapter 5—Fractals: *Moments* of shared awareness, *Meetings* of
dialogue and *Macro processes* that mobilize commitment

71

Frequently, even in strategic meetings, we plan activities in the late afternoon or evening to facilitate the strengthening of trusting relationships. The lightest touch are fun activities such as a fine dinner or even bowling or boating. Next on the continuum are a variety of self-disclosure tools. The participants can come to learn who each of their colleagues is on a deeper level. Instruments such as the Myers Briggs, that identify thinking styles, are received well by most client groups. It can produce insights such as "now I know why he or she operates that way in meetings." Exercises such as telling each other the stories of their lives also helps build trust and personal connections. "We've worked together for years and I am happy that I finally learned that about my colleague, X." Physical activities such as shadow martial arts, singing or dancing are followed by debriefing sessions that explore the emotions that emerged for each individual. Clients gain personal insight on their own feelings and behavior and come to know their colleagues in new and deeper ways, as well.

Finally, mutual feedback sessions between and among members of the team are especially helpful with teams where trust is low and team functioning is poor. Individuals receive feedback on the impact, often unintended, that their behavior has on their colleagues. We facilitate the feedback process strictly according to the ground rules of relational dialogue in order to optimize learning and protect individuals from emotional hurt.

The meeting concludes with a summary of the decisions made, as well as a debriefing on the process: what worked well and what could be improved in the strategic and/or relational dialogue process. Finally, the facilitator guides the team to draft a brief summary of the meeting for communication to the wider organization: What did we do? What did we decide? How significant was it? The method of creating the brief summary is simple: either each individual team member, or small groups of team members draft their own communication summary. This is typically done in 5-10 minutes. Then, in sequence, each team member or sub-group reports on their summary. The facilitator records each report real time on the computer that is projected onto the screen. The one ground rule in the reports is that each successive report may only include new material—no redundancies are allowed. The entire process of creating the communication summary typically takes twenty minutes. After the meeting is concluded, the facilitator synthesizes all the reports into one communication summary of the meeting and sends it to the leader who in turn sends it out to the wider organization.

Facilitating the Dialogue in Meetings

The facilitator's prime objective is to help the team achieve the purpose and goals of the meeting and in so doing, accomplish the entire agenda. There are several reasons for striving for completion of the agenda. First, the agenda has become a contract between and among the leader, the participants and the facilitator. Everyone has become invested in the agenda through their involvement in its preparation. Not to finish the entire agenda would be felt as a disappointment, at least by some. Secondly, accomplishing the entire agenda is frequently considered outside the norm of many meetings where the agenda is too packed and items are left without being addressed. Finishing the entire agenda is considered efficient and generates a positive feeling of accomplishment. Finally, within the context of the macro process, the outputs of one meeting are typically inputs to the next. Accomplishing the entire agenda of one meeting supports momentum in the entire macro process of transformation.

In support of a realistic agenda design, with appropriate time allocated to agenda topics and exercises such as sub-group discussions, the facilitator also serves as the time keeper. When decisions are required, the facilitator may also utilize a mini agenda with time allocations of five-fifteen minute segments while applying the Consultative Consensus decision making model. For example, a topic may be opened with the question on the agenda and the interview data. Five-ten minutes may be allocated for questions of clarification. Fifteen minutes in total may be allocated for each participant to share their opinion in one-two minutes each. Twenty minutes may be allocated to open discussion and debate. Ten minutes may be allocated to test the level of consensus in the team with each person declaring their position. Finally, five minutes may be allocated to the leader to make the ultimate decision.

For inexperienced or dysfunctional teams we didactically instruct team members on the stages of a decision making process. We then refer to the chart as we facilitate the process. This helps address a common pitfall

of management team meetings: premature decision making that results
in poor implementation due to the absence of shared understanding,
ownership and commitment to the decision.

The Phases of the Decision Making Process

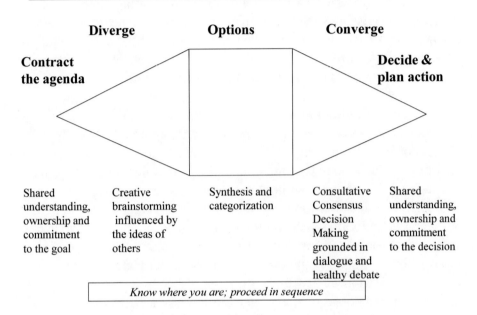

The start of the decision making process frequently occurs before
the meeting begins during the agenda design phase. The result is an
agenda-contract, agreed by the leader, the participants and the facilitator
that defines the question(s) to be answered. An agenda contract
contributes to shared understanding, ownership and commitment to the
goal of the meeting as well as to the decisions that are made.

The next phase of the meeting is typically the easiest part, divergence.
Everyone's ideas are welcome. Each person's creativity is encouraged.
This is not the time for debate. Team members are also challenged to
be open to be influenced by the ideas of others. The creative discussion
ideally becomes infectious.

The third phase of the meeting entails synthesizing and categorizing
the creative ideas to shape options for the ultimate decision. Synthesis
is most efficiently and effectively carried out by one person or a small

group. The facilitator invites one or two persons from the team to assist in the process while the other members take a break.

The next phase is the converging phase. In our experience this is typically the most difficult phase until the team has become experienced with the Consultative Consensus model of decision making. The facilitator guides the discussion such that each member's voice is heard. In strategic discussions, the facilitator may also choose to scribe the discussion on the computer for projection onto the screen as a support for the team to track on many points being stated in a short period of time.

Intermittently, the facilitator halts the discussion and summarizes what has been said and/or highlights points of disagreement that may be glossed over in the rapidity of the discussion. It is usually beneficial to the ultimate decision to take the time to focus on points of disagreement. Through healthy debate, without rancor, the team can discover the pros and cons of a decision more fully. While disagreement may be hottest between two individuals, the facilitator intervenes in the bilateral debate after a few rounds to involve the rest of the team. There are several reasons for doing so. If the other members of the team are not invited into the discussion at that time, they might become disengaged if the two pursue their disagreement over too lengthy a period of time. And the other members of the team often have new perspectives and can shed light on the disagreement. Finally, by hearing from all team members the disagreement typically dissolves into consensus.

The final phase is the decision itself. The facilitator will survey the team members so each can declare their personal opinion. The consensus is duly noted and the leader ultimately decides, either with the majority, with the minority, with a third, personal view or to postpone the decision for further study.

Facilitating the moments of awareness

Moments of awareness are insights that occur for an individual or a group when important dynamics, either strategic or relational, which have been out of awareness now become apparent. The facilitator supports and guides the process of the meeting by employing multiple means to facilitate these moments of awareness. These moments serve as fractals

Chapter 5—Fractals: *Moments* of shared awareness, *Meetings* of
dialogue and *Macro processes* that mobilize commitment

75

of the meeting and the macro process. They result in unleashed energy
to act and contribute to the goals of the meeting and the overall purpose
of the macro process.

Describing a pattern of behavior

One type of facilitating awareness entails *describing a pattern of the client's
behavior* that heretofore has been outside of awareness. In Gestalt the pattern
is called a "figure". The facilitator may introduce the new figure with a
question: "Am I the only one who sees . . . ?" This kind of intervention can
be used to help the client become aware of their own process of discussion
and decision making. The facilitator may continue for example, "While I
know you have all agreed to the ground rules of dialogue, at this time I hear
person's X, Y and Z stating their positions clearly and forcefully without
acknowledging one another or without inquiring of each other, 'what do
you think of that?'" Or, as another example, "I see that you have tried to
express your opinion several times and each time someone has interrupted
you. Your expression and body language suggest that you don't feel so
good about that. How do you feel?" Or, "I see that you have been silent for
some time, would you like to contribute your opinion?"

Another way to describe the figure, which is central to the methodologies
of the Gestalt International Study Center and the field of appreciative
inquiry, is to ask for a description of what is going well in the client
system. As this technique repeatedly has shown the client(s) become
spontaneously more open to take on and creatively solve their problems
once they have the awareness of what is going well in the system.

The facilitator also listens for paradoxical statements: "You said x which
seemed to contradict when you said y". For example, "you have stated
that this issue is a high priority for you and you are frustrated by the
behavior of a colleague whom you have stated has not delivered on certain
commitments, yet you also acknowledge that you have not read all of
the necessary material pertaining to this issue. That seems paradoxical.
What do you think of this observation?" The individual may then respond,
"I've been frustrated. I thought my colleague would have delivered on
the commitments—it's less my responsibility. That's why I haven't read
everything." This encounter opens the door to relational dialogue. The
other colleague may then respond with another perception and perhaps
frustration with the first colleague. As the mutual feedback proceeds,

possibly facilitated by the facilitator, both parties eventually can come to a new awareness of their mutual responsibilities going forward.

Posing questions

Another way of facilitating awareness entails *posing questions* such that the clients discover for themselves the new figure or pattern. In our strategic ground rules (Chapter 2), "Make explicit what have been implicit assumptions", a number of questions can facilitate awareness. Highlight key words that people employ with different meanings, "I hear each of you use the important word, X, can you each define what you mean by it?" Frequently, the members discover that they are using the same word with different meanings that contributes to friction. The awareness of the difference results in greater mutual understanding. For forceful assertions, presented as givens, a simple useful question would be "Why?" multiple times. This process helps the speaker and others gain awareness of the reasons behind the forceful assertion. Alternatively, the question may be, "What are the assumptions behind your judgment about that?" And, "How can we test that assumption as a hypothesis?"

Questions can also be used to open the clients to disclose important ideas and/or feelings and engage the clients to improve their own process rather than dwelling entirely in the content. Examples include the following:

"Is there something you are thinking of saying that you are not saying?"

"Where do you think we are now in the discussion?"

"How do you feel right now? What is happening to your energy?"

"What do you want from me as the facilitator?"

"How do you suggest we proceed? I'm not sure what is best right now."

The facilitator who acknowledges not knowing, can help catalyze energy in the client system. These kinds of questions help redirect awareness from a discussion of content only, to engaging the clients to improve their own process.

Proposing an experiment

The facilitator may also suggest that the clients engage in new behavior, what Gestalt practitioners refer to as an *experiment*. The new behavior, upon reflection, often produces new awareness. In our practice, with management teams, the experiments we sometimes use include guided

Chapter 5—Fractals: *Moments* of shared awareness, *Meetings* of
dialogue and *Macro processes* that mobilize commitment

77

shadow martial arts, singing, dance or yoga. After the experiment, the
clients are encouraged to share the emotional experience they had with
their colleagues. The frequent result is increased self awareness. For
example, the martial arts exercise may trigger emotions of anger or fear in
a competitive situation. In the ensuing discussion the client may discover
how these emotions affect his or her behavior in the workplace. With
the new awareness, the client begins a process of changing unwanted,
counter-productive behaviors. As a consequence of the self-disclosure,
the discussion also contributes to strengthened relationships in the team.

Modulating the pace

Facilitating awareness may also be supported by modulating the *pace* of
the conversation. For example, we may slow down a rapid conversation
where many are talking and few seem to be listening to one another.
This intervention may be coupled with a question to guide the clients
to look at their process and their emotions, such as "What is going
on for you right now? Take a few quiet minutes before responding."
This kind of intervention can create space for the clients to experience
self-discovery. Or, "Can you paraphrase what your colleague has just
said?" It is not uncommon that the engaged talker cannot. This can result
in a recapitulation and deeper listening than before.

Intervening in conflict

A particularly challenging moment to facilitate is when passions run high,
people are in conflict, express hostile remarks or demonstrate disrespectful
non-verbal behavior such as contemptuous expressions. The facilitator can
help resolve the conflict by employing any or all of the above techniques
so the clients can gain awareness of the process of their conflict and its
underlying reasons. One initial intervention would be to "separate the
combatants" and use one's self as facilitator to take the floor and call for a
"time out". Next, the facilitator may call upon other members of the team
to provide their feedback in response to such questions as, "How are you
feeling?" "What is going on?" "What are the underlying reasons?" In this
manner the conflict is shifted from the intransigence of those directly in
the conflict to the support of the entire team.

The facilitator may also bring attention to themes or figures that
are important to the process and are rarely discussed, such as power
and influence, particularly. "How are you using your power in this

conversation?" Or the facilitator may give the antagonists direct feedback by quoting their remarks and sharing his or her own experience, "When you said X it felt to me like you dismissing or threatening your colleague. What do you think?" Or to the leader, "When you said Y it seemed to me that you were prematurely influencing the outcome of the dialogue and quashing creative input. What do you think?"

Summary—facilitating moments of awareness

The facilitator has multiple means to facilitate moments of awareness in the client system.

One entails describing for the clients a pattern of their behavior, a figure that heretofore had been outside of awareness. The pattern or figure may be dysfunctional behavior, it may be the strengths of the system, or it may be paradoxes.

The facilitator may also pose questions such that the clients discover for themselves the new figure. These questions can be directed at helping the clients explore underlying assumptions; express previously unexpressed emotions; or examine their process of dialogue, problem solving and decision making.

Inviting the clients to experiment with new behavior and reflect on their personal emotional reactions can also support awareness. Their self-disclosures with their colleagues frequently result in increased self awareness and strengthened relationships in the team.

The facilitator may also support awareness and self discovery by modulating the pace—slowing it down to allow reflection or speeding it up to achieve closure and the objectives of the meeting.

Finally, the facilitator may help resolve conflict by employing any or all of the above techniques in order to help the clients gain awareness of the process of their conflict and its underlying reasons. The facilitator can use his or her personal presence to take the floor and redirect the conversation from conflict to reflection, including an invitation to other members of the team to participate.

Chapter 5—Fractals: *Moments* of shared awareness, *Meetings* of dialogue and *Macro processes* that mobilize commitment

79

Examples of facilitating moments of awareness from Genesis cases (Section 2)

Introduction
The examples that follow focus only on facilitating moments even though this chapter addresses facilitation of moments, meeting and the macro process. The reason is that the Genesis cases presented in Section 2 exhaustively describe the facilitation of two macro processes and two specific meetings. Embedded in those cases are multiple moments of facilitation. This section extracts some of those moments to illustrate three common and robust types of facilitation of moments:
- feedback of the pattern of behavior
- questioning
- proposing an experiment

Globalization
A moment of awareness catalyzed by feedback of the pattern of behavior
In the process of globalizing the Division I Purchasing Organization of the multinational corporation, MNX, several of the participants had difficulty making the shift from their traditional regional roles to the new global roles that they were expected to assume. One of the regional buyers who had had the most difficulty adjusting to the global role had repeatedly tried to renege on commitments taken in prior meetings. When Michael presented notes of those prior meetings that clearly showed verbatim what he had previously said, he conceded that he had previously been in agreement. By his concession to the prior agreements, the team was able to proceed beyond his resistance to shared awareness of what everyone needed to do in the process of globalization.

The verbatim feedback described the "figure". The resistor became aware in the moment that he—and everyone else—was accountable for prior agreements; each meeting was important and the outputs of one meeting were indeed inputs for the next one. The entire team shared in the awareness and become even more focused, disciplined and committed to the integrity of their process of dialogue and decision making. The moment also contributed to the shared awareness of the whole team on what they had to do to globalize their purchasing operation. The moment had confirmed the objective of the individual meetings and the macro process: to globalize the processes and roles of purchasing managers.

Overcoming conflicts in a merger
A moment of awareness catalyzed by questions

The integration of two companies, the acquirer, Euro Corp and the acquired, ABC, as described in Chapter 14, Merger Integration, began with a meeting with the leadership teams of the two merging companies. The meeting had the objective of designing the framework of the new company. Once again, we would utilize the Genesis Urgent Vision model (see Chapter 8 for a full definition).

In the days before the first meeting, serving as the facilitator, I conducted a series of interviews with each member of the two teams. My questions aimed to ascertain their hopes and expectations for the new merged company. I planned to use the interview data as input to the meeting. I discovered that during the early months of the merger integration process deep misunderstandings had arisen between the two leadership teams. Mary had recently been hired to replace the former CEO who had been forced to resign by the Board of Directors in the face of the initial problems with the merger.

Mary and I had agreed to commence the first meeting by addressing the barriers to trust that had arisen between the members of the leadership teams of the two merging companies. I invited each individual to tell his or her story of what had occurred during the early months of the attempted integration. With growing irritation, one Euro Corp manager described the behavior of the former CEO of ABC. The Euro Corp manager had concluded that the former ABC CEO had attempted to make a private deal with the former CEO of Euro Corp. The moment was tense. I facilitated the moment by asking the former ABC CEO to respond. He had not sought a private deal, he explained. I asked the Euro Corp manager to respond and while he acknowledged that he had made unsubstantiated assumptions, his body language suggested that he held to his opinion.

Then I invited the two to talk privately with each other before the dinner at the end of the first day; as part of the meeting design, pairs of managers, one from each of the merging companies, would also be similarly invited. Both managers later acknowledged that by having surfaced the conflicting perceptions in the open meeting of the two former leadership teams that they had proceeded to make progress in developing a constructive relationship going forward during their subsequent one on one meeting. A new collaborative figure of their

Chapter 5—Fractals: *Moments* of shared awareness, *Meetings* of
dialogue and *Macro processes* that mobilize commitment

81

relationship had begun to emerge. They wanted to make the effort since
they both would be colleagues in the new leadership team.

The next phase of the meeting addressed each of the dimensions of
the Genesis Urgent Vision model. Step by step the participants worked
their way through each dimension utilizing dialogue and healthy
debate while referring to the notes from the interviews both with hard
copy and projection onto the screen. Following the precept that form
follows function, the topic of structure was addressed last. Based on the
interviews I had conducted, we had several draft organization designs on
the table for discussion, including one preferred by the CEO, Mary. Her
design represented a significant departure from the structure of each of
the two companies before the merger.

The participants explored the new structures in terms of strengths
and weaknesses, until a consensus emerged that favored the Mary's
recommendation. The former Euro Corp managers all supported the new
structure. Yet, even in agreement with the end result, the former ABC
team initially hedged and expressed their reluctance. While logically,
they had no argument with it, emotionally, they were not ready to accept
it. The moment was tense. This could have been a critical impasse. If
they didn't agree, the options were not clear. Would the CEO decide
to approve the structure without their consent? If so, would the ABC
managers quit? Would the CEO convene more meetings to explore
alternatives? The time for the meeting was running out. Members had
to leave on time to catch planes back to their home countries.

I suggested that the ABC team meet by themselves to answer the
question as to whether or not they could support the implementation of
the new design or would they want to propose yet another alternative.
Since we were within hours of adjourning and people leaving to catch
flights, I asked the ABC team to conclude their deliberations in twenty
minutes. Upon their return, they announced that they would accept the
new organization. Relief swept the room. The ABC managers explained
that they had felt heard by the new CEO and the colleagues of the former
Euro Corp and that all their questions and doubts had been expressed and
addressed during the meeting. As one ABC manager put it, "we turned
over every stone and this new structure does make the most sense, even
though we tried to find its weaknesses. We will give it a try."

The ABC leadership team had arrived at a moment of shared awareness that they could and would participate and implement the new organization. They had been parties to its design and they now were in agreement with their new colleagues, the former Euro Corp managers. The moment confirmed the objective of the meeting—the overall framework for the new Euro Corp had been designed and agreed. The moment also represented a key first step in accomplishing the goals of the macro process—the detailed design and implementation of the new Euro Corp organization. The leadership teams of the two former companies had come together, addressed past conflicts, made progress in building trust and agreed on the framework of their new organization. The next set of meetings, first with the new leadership team and later at a Leadership Conference with top 3-4 levels of management, would add important details to the organizational framework that they had created.

Discovering healthy friction
A moment of awareness catalyzed by an experiment
In the case, Long Term Improvement (Chapter 11), Arri engaged his clients periodically in experimental behavior to help them discover the benefits of friction in an organization, i.e., "healthy friction". Through healthy friction, different views are explored, constructive conflicts are addressed and frequently, creative solutions are found. As one of the experiments Arri introduced the participants to martial arts exercises. With the guidance of a psychologist-martial arts instructor, the participants, with protective padding, actually engaged in contact.

In debriefing the experience with the clients, Arri facilitated their discovery of the emotional reactions they had had to the conflict, such as fear and anger. He also facilitated their discovery of the benefits of healthy friction as a process of using competition to solve problems and improve performance. Through further discussions, the clients discovered that in virtually all decision making processes, within the organization, there are competing interests that are the cause of conflict. When the conflict or friction is explored thoroughly through dialogue, the result can be decisions that account properly and beneficially for the competing interests involved. If the conflict is avoided, the decisions are sub-optimal. If the conflict turns acrimonious then dysfunctional behaviors emerge that can disrupt the decision making and execution process.

Chapter 5—Fractals: *Moments* of shared awareness, *Meetings* of
dialogue and *Macro processes* that mobilize commitment

83

Lessons in facilitating moments of shared awareness, meetings of dialogue and macro processes that mobilize commitment

The facilitator is aware of multiple dimensions simultaneously:

- Supporting moments of awareness through questions, experiments or by offering a new "figure" to consider.
- Tracking the quality of the strategic and/or relational dialogue in meetings and intervening, when appropriate, to help the client system become more effective in its dialogue and in finding shared awareness and understanding on critical issues.
- Supporting the clients to accomplish their objectives within the available time as set forth in the agenda contributes to developing trust with the clients.
- Being aware of the goals of the macro process to mobilize commitment across the entire organization and during the meeting or at its conclusion, intervening with questions and suggestions on how to proceed with the macro process: as planned, or with modifications based on discoveries that may have arisen in the meeting.
- Distinguishing between the process and the content.
- Having familiarity with the content questions that are most important to the clients; and highlighting for the clients conflicts and inconsistencies in content positions in need of resolution.
- Facilitating the moments, meetings and macro process in partnership with the leader/client who leads the decision making and is the ultimate judge of the quality of the content.

Chapter 6
Boundaries: Freedom within a Framework

The VP had raised questions with me in a coaching session:

"I'm concerned. I've been asked by the CEO to lead a process to develop a strategic recommendation for the Board, with consultation from staff. What's my role? While the Board is the ultimate decision maker, do we make decisions during the consultation process? If so, who is the decision maker? How do I deal with the possibility that staff may want to challenge strategy? I want to be open and yet I want the discussions to be focused on the question at hand."

I asked the VP, "What is the Board expecting? Have they made any decisions with regard to this strategic question?"

The VP answered, "The Board is expecting a strategy that can be implemented and they want input from staff in the hopes that the staff will enthusiastically support its implementation. They have already decided on the direction. This is a strategic direction for that they want us staff to develop more specifics."

"And what is your CEO expecting?" I asked.

"The CEO would like me to present a detailed proposal for the strategy to the Management Team and him, based on the rounds of consultation with the staff. Ultimately, the CEO will make the proposal to the Board," he answered. *"The CEO is also expecting that I learn to develop strategy in a consultative fashion through this experience."*

As we talked together we developed the schema for a process of consultation. First we addressed his question regarding what his role would be. I recommended that he would play the role of leader of a series of "focus group" discussions with clusters of staff members. He would introduce the decision already taken by the Board that the organization would enter a new area of activity and needed a strategy to specify how it would be implemented. He would explain that the purpose of the focus group would be to brainstorm and explore what that strategy should entail. In response to his speculation that the staff may challenge the strategy, I answered that he needed to be clear: the focus group would

NOT be asked whether or not the organization should enter this new area of activity. That decision had already been made by the Board.

I also suggested that the VP's role would be to take the inputs from the various focus group sessions and formulate a recommendation to the CEO and the Management Team. In this capacity his role would be the "decision maker" of what the recommendation would contain. The CEO had empowered him with that discretionary authority. He would not only be a facilitator of the focus group discussions; he would also be expected to add his judgment in synthesizing what he heard.

His recommendation would be presented to The Management Team, who would, in turn, review and modify it as they saw fit; the CEO would ultimately decide on the final recommendation for the Board. After the Board made its final decision and budget allocation, then the CEO and every member of the Management Team would develop operating plans in order to deliver the strategy in the next year(s).

I explained that the VP had an opportunity to apply the principle of "freedom within a framework". The focus groups would have the freedom to express their views any way they saw fit, within the parameters as presented by the VP and as agreed by the CEO and the management team. "In my experience with similar situations, the focus groups will appreciate being consulted, be stimulated by the challenge to be creative and will be comfortable with the clarity of being guided by what they may and may not discuss," I added. I also reviewed the consultative decision making ground rules (Chapter 2, above) that I had introduced to the VP and his colleagues at a prior meeting, and suggested he employ them in the focus groups. This way he could clarify that the role of the focus group members was to brainstorm and strive for consensus on leading ideas and that his role was as the ultimate decision maker of what the recommendation to the CEO and Management Team would contain.
The VP concluded the meeting with a smile, "This all makes good sense."

This intervention felt seamless and straightforward to me. The VP was seeking guidance and was open. The context enabled the conversation. I had been consulting with him and his colleagues on the management team in order to open the organizational culture for deeper dialogue, enhanced trust, more creative problem solving and more inclusive decision making. He and I had also had a prior individual coaching session. He was eager to learn to strengthen his own leadership abilities. He was relatively new in his position and had a number of direct reports and a complex agenda of objectives.

As we talked through his questions and I shared my suggestions, they served as a new figure for him. The concept of freedom within a framework, the role he could play and the process he could guide all seemed to click. He became aware of how he could manage his new challenge. He appeared energized at the end of the conversation.

Freedom within a framework

The individual or team has the *freedom* to make decisions within the *framework* already decided by higher authority. The principle of freedom within a framework is often experienced as clarifying and liberating in the design of the macro process of organizational transformation. It helps simplify and make manageable a multi faceted transformation process in an organization with all of its complexities by orienting everyone to the value added work that each can contribute. The framework defines boundaries of responsibility, authority, accountability and where they are shared with others. It provides clarity on what is given, what is non-negotiable, what is open and what needs to be decided. Each one has freedom within the rules and norms of the organization and within the decisions made by higher authority regarding the framework.

There are risks with the principle. Frameworks may be perceived as constraining, rigid or not worthy of acceptance. This can be avoided by creating opportunities for bottom up feedback during the macro process before senior management finalizes the framework for the transformation process. And if individuals don't agree with the emerging framework, they have the opportunity to challenge it. Sometimes, this requires courage. Freedom can also be abused. Individuals may not understand the boundaries within which they are expected to work. Conflict over who is responsible for what can arise, that can be destructive. This risk can be avoided or mitigated by guiding the inevitable conflict into healthy debate, within the ground rules of strategic and relational dialogue.

The VP was relieved to see how he could lead the process of consultation and how others in the organization could be clearly and appropriately invited to contribute. The principle of freedom within a framework helps set the boundaries of dialogue for each level of the hierarchy and affords clarity regarding the roles that each level and each manager plays. The top of the hierarchy, the CEO and the management team, have the key leadership role to determine transformation frameworks, such as strategic direction, values, policies, processes, etc. and delegate to next level teams the development of details, such as operational plans and direct responsibility for implementation. In an organizational culture where free and informed choice is valued, individuals tend to be motivated and assume responsibility and accountability for their own contributions to implementation. The application of this principle supports continuous improvements, innovation and productivity while providing an antidote for micro management.

There are many familiar examples of this principle. A jazz group improvises within the framework of the rhythm and the key. A soccer team improvises within the framework of the positions to which players are assigned and the knowledge they have of each other's capabilities. A business team improvises creative solutions within the framework of strategic goals they have agreed to achieve.

Working within a framework requires discipline grounded in practice, methods and tools. Improvisation requires freedom to experiment within the given framework. Creativity can also mean re-inventing the framework altogether. The re-invention of the frameworks themselves may refer to the establishment of fundamentally new business models, strategies, business processes, structures or culture. This work of re-invention requires the deep work of re-examining the underlying assumptions of the current modus operandi, what Argyris calls Model II or double loop learning thinking.

Example of experiencing freedom within a framework from Genesis cases (Section 2)

The CEO had established a strategic framework to expand the company's presence in the China market aggressively, as introduced above in Chapter 3 and described in full in Chapter 13, *Accelerated Strategy*

Development. He convened a team to develop the details of the strategy within that framework. The framework provided the boundaries within which the participants would have the freedom to contribute their knowledge, expertise and creativity in the development of the strategy.

Kees proposed and the clients readily agreed to have a preparatory design meeting which would more fully define the CEO's strategic framework as well as prepare other details of the larger planning meeting to follow. The design meeting included the senior management teams of both sister companies: HMM and Q&I, including the two CEOs, MJ and RDG.

With the meeting one month away, Kees facilitated the design meeting. In addition to specifying the framework and goals for the China strategy, the objectives of the design meeting included the following:

- Define the objectives of the meeting
- Define the scope of the meeting
- Define the methodology, ground rules, agenda and input documents for the meeting
- Decide the participants and roles
- Decide the venue and dates
- Prepare the communications to participants in preparation for the meeting

Goals for the strategy

The CEO opened the preparatory meeting by reiterating the challenging goals for the development of the China Growth strategy:

- Grow the business to 500 million USD of sales within China in five years, more than 3 times the current sales volume
- Become an independent business region within the HMM, Inc. structure by FY 07, that is "spin-off" from being under the aegis of the HMM, Inc. Eurasia Region
- Become the primary source for components, sub-assemblies and certain OE machines for HHM's worldwide operations. This goal illustrates HHM's long term commitment to doing business in China. This commitment would be seen by the Chinese market as a powerful gesture of good citizenship and

would support HHM's bid to obtain a license to continue to operate in China
- Protect HHM's proprietary knowledge

Goal of the Meeting
The CEO stated that the objective of the meeting would be to develop a preliminary strategic plan and action plan to finalize the strategic plan within 90 days. The strategy needed to be financially robust in order to justify the anticipated significant capital and personnel investments to be made.

Scope of the Meeting
To assure clarity and focus on such a complex topic, the participants developed which questions would be in scope, as well as out of scope during the meeting.

Methodology, ground rules, agenda and input documents for the meeting
Kees proposed a simple methodology that would form the basis for the 3 day agenda and which he had employed over the years in multiple meetings, with similar constraints and conditions, with consistent success:
What are our objectives?
What is the current reality?
What is our desired state?
What actions do we need to achieve the desired state?

There were risks with this methodology. The participants would be asked to work in ways that were foreign to them. In the more conventional business strategy processes it is common that the marketing strategy is developed first and then is used as input to the other strategies sequentially, including manufacturing, sourcing, HR, finance, IT, R&D, etc. over months. As needed, the cycle is repeated to achieve alignment among all the components. Given the constraints of 3 days for the meeting, these conventional approaches would not work. Instead, the different functional disciplines would have to work in parallel rather than in sequence to develop their component strategic plans. The danger is that the different strategies could evolve into conflict with one another and the exercise could fail. Kees and his clients hoped and trusted that the participants would be willing to work in this unconventional manner and that the resultant different functional plans would fit together sufficiently that the participants would feel motivated by their agreements to proceed with detailed planning and implementation.

To support the limited time for developing the preliminary strategic plans, Kees proposed to the project manager to consider the development of input documents in a few priority topic areas. While brief, the documents would serve to help orient the participants to the conversation and help accelerate the dialogue by providing baseline data and codification of existing ideas held by management. They were to be considered catalysts for the dialogue, not formal proposals. With a preparatory team, Kees facilitated the making of a draft sourcing strategy based on the project manager's knowledge plus the input of a few sourcing and manufacturing managers. The project manager prepared a draft of a 5-year sales outlook based on his own knowledge and the input of a few marketing managers. Kees knew that by preparing the draft document not only was he providing a useful tool for the meeting, he was also educating himself on an important content question that would enable him to be even more effective as a facilitator. He would really understand what the clients were discussing. For the same reason, later he also studied the clients' preliminary financial model that ultimately would be core to the final China strategic plan.

Kees also proposed that the ground rules for the meeting should be explicit (see above, Chapter 2, Strategic Dialogue Ground Rules). Given that the meeting team would have to work fast without the benefit of prepared data and analysis, he further proposed the lead ground rule would be "vigor over rigor". *This meant that the knowledge and judgment of all assembled on the team would be required and trusted. The participants had the freedom within the framework to develop the strategy themselves.* There would be no time, nor need, during the 3 days for additional data and analysis. By making the ground rule explicit, Kees also contracted with the group that in his capacity as facilitator, he would champion vigor over rigor. If any managers were reluctant to proceed without more data, Kees would challenge them to trust their own judgment, knowledge and experience. He would remind them that in 3 days they could and would develop the framework for the China

Growth strategy. During the following 90 days, there would be time to fill in the details with more data and analysis, as needed.

Participants and roles
The participants for the meeting were selected based on the criterion that those with the lead responsibility for the eventual implementation of the strategy across the various functional departments and geographies would collaboratively develop the strategy. With this in mind, the participants who were invited comprised eighteen (18) people, including a balance of Chinese, British, Americans, Australians, Canadians and Swedes represented Sales/Marketing, Finance, IT, Operations, Human Resources, Supply Chain, Engineering, Quality and Human Resources.

The project leader would serve as the ultimate decision maker in the room, when the consensus process required his intervention and Kees would serve as the facilitator of the process of the meeting dialogue.

In addition, the two sponsors, the CEOs of HMM and Q&I, and their two entire management teams would also join at different times. Their collective role would be to sign off on the strategy and assure that all resources necessary would be made available. They would also serve as enablers of implementation. If and when roadblocks emerged and competing priorities would have to be resolved, the CEOs and members of their management teams would step in, as necessary. At the beginning of the meeting the CEOs would present the framework (the goals and scope) of the exercise to the participants and entertain questions. And at the end of the meeting they would act as ultimate decision makers of the proposed strategy. The process worked. By exercising the freedom within the framework and by experiencing the active support and participation of senior management, the participants succeeded in achieving the goals and objectives of the meeting. They developed the next evolution of the strategy and their commitment had been mobilized.

Lessons in establishing boundaries: freedom within a framework

The first phase of the macro process of transformation ideally is a series of meetings in which the senior team will establish the holistic framework for the transformation with shared understanding, buy-in and commitment. The framework has two components—the process and the content. The content comprises the business objectives to be achieved. The process comprises how the transformation will proceed.

The sequence of macro process steps continues to be based on trust. The process engages ever wider concentric rings of the organization to participate in the dialogue, co-design the solutions and fill in the details of the framework established by the leadership team. The macro process manifests the principle of freedom within the framework.

Chapter 7
Multiplier affects: Leveraging Total Resources and Strengthening Individual Capability and Performance

"I have a brilliant brand marketing manager working here in Brazil who should serve all of Latin America. He's got the knowledge, the smarts and the talent. Currently, each country has its own brand marketing manager and none of them are at his level. If he led brand marketing across the region, the performance and results in all markets would improve without a doubt. Furthermore, it will be a great learning experience for him. He'll learn how to negotiate with multiple organizations and a variety of market segments. It will stretch him strategically and interpersonally."

We were talking about the project of integrating all of the Latin American countries into one regional entity. He was expressing his enthusiastic support for the organizational transformation that he and his colleagues were embarking upon with the assistance of Arri and me, as consultants. In a recent prior meeting with approximately 25 top leaders from all of the country organizations, we had led them through the process of designing their top level operating framework. Before the team actually engaged in defining what their new structure would look like, we led the team through the process of defining the other elements of the model (see above) plus an exercise to define their "organization design principles". One of the principles they embraced was "leverage total resources and strengthen individual capability and performance". The VP's impassioned vision for the future potential of the brand marketing manager, described above, would be realized within the implementation of the new regional organization. It exemplified the principle that his knowledge and expertise would be leveraged across all countries for the benefit of the total business and in the process he would have a powerful professional development experience, as well.

I felt happy and comfortable with the VP. He shared the awareness with me that the regionalization process should be grounded in the principle of leveraging the totality and strengthening the individual. He felt like an ally with the complex process on which we had embarked. He was a champion of regionalization. He knew that the business results would improve by leveraging the resources, including talented people like the brand marketing manager whom he wanted to promote. He also believed that talented people with expanded responsibilities would grow professionally, as well. I experienced the happiness of shared awareness with another human being on a matter of importance to both of us plus the optimism that, with his support, the overall process would proceed well.

Leveraging total resources and strengthening individual capability and performance

Groups and organizations exist to accomplish goals that individuals cannot accomplish on their own. This entails optimizing cooperation and has two principle dimensions: leveraging total resources and strengthening individual capability and performance. Leveraging means that the impact of a force can be multiplied. Leveraging total resources, including people, know-how, money, assets and technology, is a characteristic of effective organizations that continually improve their productivity.

Strengthening individual capability and performance is the companion process. Every team member has the responsibility to cooperate with fellow teammates to leverage collective impact while continually improving personal performance to contribute to the collective impact. The principle of leveraging total resources while strengthening individual capability and performance is a key criterion of how leaders carry out one of their prime responsibilities: the allocation of resources for optimal results.

In the example above, one person was redeployed so that his knowledge and expertise could be leveraged to reach more people and corners of the organization. Analogously, effective global brands are leveraged such that the investment in developing and marketing the brand is applied across vast markets. The ROI is far greater than having a multiplicity of local brands requiring multiple parallel investments.

Dialogue can also produce leverage effects. In one particular project I worked on, the Order to Delivery process was considered too slow and error prone by customers. The people with responsibility for different sub-processes, such as order entry, logistics, manufacturing, warehousing, distribution, etc. experienced stress, friction, confusion and low trust with one another. The small, well focused action I employed was simply to bring the people together, face to face, to improve their process. Many had never even met each other previously, although they were interdependent. The meeting employed strategic dialogue to clarify the decision making process and eliminate non-value added steps in the overall Order to Delivery Process. Even without explicit relational dialogue, the trust among the participants increased by simply working together to improve their shared process in the same room. The result was a dramatic reduction in the cycle time from order to delivery, fewer errors, happier customers and significant cost savings realized on the bottom line.

Interwoven with leveraging the totality, the process of strengthening the capability and performance of each individual member also strengthens the organizational system as a whole. The participants in the Order to Delivery meetings learned to strengthen their skills in dialogue and teamwork. The brand marketing manager who moved from leading Brazil to leading all of Latin America learned to expand his repertoire of professional skills, including the latest methods, knowledge and technologies to support marketing on a much larger scale. Individuals find it motivating to develop themselves while simultaneously contributing to the development of their organizations.

A basketball team can serve as a simple example. The team reviews game videos to analyze its performance and determine areas for improvement either on the level of the team as a team or on the level of each individual on the team. Next, the team practices improvements to its drills and plays. Individuals practice shooting, passing and rebounding skills to strengthen their contribution to the team. In the game, the points are scored as a result of leveraging the totality of the teamwork and the strength of the skills of the individuals. The basketball team, like a corporation develops into a "learning organization" such that each individual grows and learns and advances his or her own career capabilities while the organization develops new collective capabilities and learns as well.

The process of strengthening personal capabilities while leveraging the resources of the totality is a challenge of *balancing one's individuality with one's sense of togetherness with others.* The individual in the organization is always in relationship with others. The balancing process requires that the individual addresses personal needs simultaneously with the diverse needs of others. The individual also has personal values that are non-negotiable. If the individual is pressured by the group or superiors to violate a fundamental value such as integrity, then the individual has the choice to compromise and cave in or say, "No, either the pressure is withdrawn and I maintain my value or I leave."

Examples of leveraging total resources and strengthening individual capability and performance from Genesis cases (Section 2)

The organization design of the newly merged Greenfields Company included the creation of a central marketing unit devoted to regional strategy and country retail organizations focused on implementing those strategies through sales. This was another story within Arri's Chapter 11 case: Long-term Improvement, as introduced above, in Chapter 2. The relationship between Greenfields Central Marketing and the Country Retail Organizations had been problematic from the outset of the launch of the new structure of the newly merged company. The two units had had difficulty collaborating. Central Marketing had been seen by the Country Retail Organizations as micro-managing, continually asking for information and interfering with the Country Retail Organizations while adding hardly any value. The Country Retail Organizations had been seen by Greenfields Central Marketing as "their employees" in need of central direction.

A meeting of the two units was convened by the CEO with Arri as the facilitator. It employed strategic dialogue to seek agreement on the roles and decision making authorities in marketing between the two organizations. The focus was on how best to leverage the totality of both central and country based marketing. As the final activity for the meeting, a martial arts teacher who was also a psychologist led an exercise in low-impact contact. The purpose was to experience the interface between the two organizational units symbolically and physically. The most effective encounters in the exercise, as were revealed in the debriefing with the instructor at the conclusion, were those in which both partners who were engaged in the "fight" were present and assertive, without harming the partner. The participants experienced effective sparring as a metaphor for dialogue. The least effective encounters experienced were those in which either one party over-powered the other, both parties were somewhat passive or both parties became overly aggressive. The exercise also served another purpose: it provided a physical release from the mental work that had been consuming everyone in their discussions.

At the end, each member was invited to make personal commitments to the whole group as to how they would specifically contribute to making the interface work well in the future. This meeting was intended to mark the beginning of a new era: one of partnership between the two organizations. They committed that together they would support the growth in the market place and that their roles and competencies were to be complementary. While at the conclusion of the meeting, the participants reported that they felt they had made progress in improving the relationship between the two organizations; one year later they were still having difficulties with one another.

It was then that a new CEO had taken over and with his fresh eyes he was not satisfied with what he found as he examined the relationship between Central Marketing and the Country Retailers. While the organization design, roles and decision making authorities between the two units had been agreed during the meeting of the prior year, there still were concerns that the *behaviors of the individuals* in the various marketing organizations were still dysfunctional and agreements between individuals in the two units were still not being fulfilled. Business results and the associated performance of the individuals were seen by the CEO and others as sub-optimal with still too much friction and misunderstanding between the Central and Country units.

Once again the CEO decided to convene a meeting between the two units and asked Arri to facilitate. This time, the meeting would focus explicitly on relational dialogue. The process of carefully guided giving and receiving individual feedback provided each team member new insights about their own and one another's behaviors and the unintended impacts they were having on one another. The results, as reported by the participants, included: personal learning; stronger mutual understanding and bonding; clear "I will" commitments from individuals to change aspects of their behavior in order to foster stronger collaboration; a shared awareness of how they could strengthen their performance as marketing colleagues even though some worked in Central Marketing and some worked in the individual countries.

This meeting, grounded in relational dialogue, was reported by the members of both Central and Country Marketing to have been helpful in moving their relationship toward greater collaboration. Their strategic dialogue became more effective and the business results began to improve. The organization benefited by leveraging the total marketing resources while strengthening the capabilities of the individual managers in both Central and Country Marketing.

Lessons in leveraging total resources and strengthening individual capability and performance

Effective organizational transformation is a balance between support for individuality and support for the totality, i.e., helping individuals strengthen their capabilities while leveraging the resources of the total organization. A transformation process that has been skewed one way or the other carries risks. A primary emphasis on the totality and leveraging total resources may sacrifice the needs of individuals through dramatic actions such as drastic cost reductions and layoffs in the name of "economies of scale". The consequences can be alienation at worst, or lack luster commitment, at best.

A primary emphasis on individuals, such as training programs, may sacrifice opportunities for leverage and be too timid in leading necessary organizational changes. Individuals may learn new skills and still become frustrated that the promised organizational changes do not materialize.

Facilitation of strategic and relational dialogue, as well as coaching, supports each individual client in gaining self-awareness, learning the skills of dialogue and in becoming effective as individual managers and leaders.

At the same time, by facilitating the process of the client-teams they become more effective as teams and can then leverage the resources of the total organization.

Chapter 8
Scope: Transforming the Entire System

In the process of merging Euro Corp and ABC, introduced above (Chapter 5,) the macro design of the new organization resulted from the series of meetings with the new Leadership Team that I facilitated. After four meetings over three months, the CEO, Mary, and the Leadership Team decided that the broad framework of the organizational design was ready to be implemented. They had addressed the entire organizational system by employing the Genesis Urgent Vision Model. They had decided on the outline of an operating framework for their winning and sustainable business model, their business processes, the values that would guide their culture and their structure.

Urgent Vision

They agreed to engage the next levels of the organization to design the details by convening the Leadership Conference that Mary and

I had discussed at the inception of the process. Their subordinates would be given the freedom to design the next operational aspects of the organization design within the broad framework that they, as the Leadership Team had defined themselves.

The Leadership Team had begun to gel after the succession of meetings. They had come a long way from the mutual suspicion which had surfaced in their first meeting, months earlier. They had made a series of shared decisions with regard to the new organizational design and they had come to know each other personally through personal story telling.

In the same Leadership Team meeting in which they decided to launch implementation of the new organization with the Leadership Conference in less than a month, the members fully engaged in an exercise which I explained would hopefully support further development of trusting relationships in the team. The site was a field near a river, in a remote area, festooned with low lying plants ripe with blueberries, surrounded by birches and conifers. The evening sun hovered, even as the days of summer were waning. Before dinner, wine was shared by all and each team member was invited to tell their personal story.

The stories became intimate revelations including troubled marriages, difficult youths and ultimately, later in the evening and back in the cabin, the grief still felt for parents who had died in recent years. The intimacy had a transformative impact on the team; the increased trust was almost palpable. At least one member acknowledged nearly one year later that through these exchanges he discovered in himself emotions and values that, until then, had been outside his immediate awareness. Mary and other members of the Leadership Team later reported that they felt that his effectiveness as a leader had also strengthened over the period.

As the decision was made to proceed rapidly with the Leadership Conference I had mixed emotions. I was happy that the CEO and the Leadership Team had overcome their initial mutual suspicion, found momentum and had come to agreement on their organization design. And I was struck by the openness of their personal stories. At the same time, I wondered if they were ready for implementation. Would the managers of the acquired company, ABC, be able to lead the significant changes on the ground, given that for years they had managed a structure and business model that had been dramatically different? Would the CEO provide sufficient support to her managers or continue to adopt the common corporate leadership attitude: "just do it"?

I was sufficiently caught up in the enthusiasm of the team and the CEO that I did not challenge them on my misgivings at the time. I was delighted that so much strategic progress had been made. And while we had also made progress in helping them develop trust with one another, I, like they, remained focused on the strategic dimension. Later in the process my misgivings became more of a reality.

The Leadership Conference

The Leadership Conference included the Leadership Team and the next level managers, i.e., direct reports of the Leadership Team plus selected others. Through dialogue and further definition of the specifics, the Leadership Team intended that the participants would share understanding, buy-in and commitment to the implementation of the new Euro Corp organization.

They also acknowledged that the Leadership Conference would be one more opportunity for the Leadership Team as a unified team to strengthen their leadership of the business; they would communicate their plans for the new Euro Corp with "one voice". They gave themselves an aggressive lead time of only three weeks. The conference would comprise three full days of work, including three evenings of fun and relationship building.

Preparation

The CEO and I developed the first draft of the detailed agenda based on the outline agreed with the Leadership Team and grounded in the Genesis Urgent Vision Model. Given that the total number of participants would number 70, three of my Genesis partners joined me as facilitators.

All of us as facilitators met one on one with individual Leadership Team members to review and plan the details of the agenda's segments that pertained to their areas. This also allowed the Genesis consultants who were new to Euro Corp to begin to cultivate partnership relationships with the Leadership Team members with whom they would be working. The Leadership Team and the Genesis consultants also met together to review the entire agenda, the processes to be employed and the roles that everyone would play in the meeting. Each Leadership Team member would have a prominent role explaining one dimension of the new organization design, as a prelude to interactive exercises in which the participants would be guided to develop more of the specifics and to "add to, amend and validate" their work.

Methodology

The Leadership Conference was devoted principly to strategic dialogue. The CEO, Mary, introduced the meeting with an overview of the new Euro Corp organization and an invitation to all the participants to exercise their own freedom within the framework as developed to that point by the Leadership Team. The Genesis consultants facilitated the sub-group discussions to support this process.

The Leadership Team anticipated one especially difficult challenge in the new organization. Managers would be required to shift from a history of internal competition to a mixed model of collaboration in certain areas of work with competition in other areas. To help the managers prepare themselves for this challenge, we facilitated a simulation exercise so the participants could experience how they would manage this paradox of combining competition and collaboration in their relationships with one another.

The history of internal competition was characteristic of the prior ABC organization. Each Euro Corp country had a group of "company managing directors" who ran different "companies" with different company names all under the the umbrella of ABC. They functioned as competitors because they represented different suppliers who wanted distributors dedicated to their own interests exclusively.

In the new Euro Corp structure the entire company was being designed as one integrated organizational system. The company's managing directors would report to the SVP of the country, a new role, and not only would they be expected to continue to compete in terms of representing their respective suppliers they would also be expected to collaborate in selling to the largest customers.

The potential for sales growth through the collaboration of the companies within a country was easy to envision. One customer could purchase a complementary variety of wines and spirits from different suppliers in a single transaction with Euro Corp. Yet, the Leadership Team anticipated that changing the behavior and mindset of the company managing directors would not be easy since they had been competing with one another for years and their suppliers had grown accustomed to having their own dedicated distributors (the former ABC companies).

Instead of each company managing director viewing their small "company" as their locus of attention, the Leadership Conference was designed so that they could experience collaboration with one another and to view Euro Corp as their organization. Many participants reported that their awareness indeed had shifted from being a member of a single company within a country to being a member of Euro Corp, a European company with operations in several European countries.

During the course of the three day conference, the top managerial levels of the newly merged Euro Corp built on the work of the Leadership Team and designed the next iteration of their new organization as a total, integrated system. Through the act of collaborative design, implementation of the new organization had begun.

After the conference concluded, I rode to the airport with the CEO. We were both pleased and relieved. The conference had ended on a positive, energetic note, apparently for most everyone. She was most appreciative of the work that my Genesis partners and I had done. The feedback from the participants was overwhelmingly positive. Yet, I had the nagging concern that the complexity of the change they were embarking upon was extremely difficult. I suggested to the CEO that my partners and I should support the individual Leadership Team members in the implementation phase, especially the establishment of their new management teams in their respective countries to assure the building of trust and effectiveness within those teams.

I felt it difficult to make the argument. On the one hand, I believed the organization needed significant additional strategic and relational support with implementation, on the other hand I felt constrained that I might be perceived as promoting myself for additional business. I felt awkward in the discussion. I continued the conversation with the CEO some weeks later and the discussion remained awkward. She dismissed the need. She wanted her managers "to get on with it". While she did invite me to continue to work with the organization, the activities were limited. I felt disappointed that I had not been able to excite her with the need for more intense follow up work. A year later my misgivings began to be realized. Fractures appeared in the Leadership Team. She invited me again to work with the Leadership Team, yet she and I were unable to help them address their conflicts. The CEO went on to fire two members. Arguments broke out and results did not achieve promise.

As I write this, I now see in retrospect that while the strategic work I had done with the client helped them launch their new organization successfully, the relationship work I had done with them had been inadequate and left them with problems that they could not resolve. I had thought, at the time, that we were addressing the "whole system" of their new organization by utilizing our comprehensive Genesis approach and toolkit. Now I see that we had insufficiently addressed a fundamental dimension of their whole system—the relationships in the Leadership Team and the management teams which each member of the Leadership Team led within their own country or functional department.

Transforming the entire system

Change any one sub-system and have an impact on all other sub-systems
To lead an organizational transformation effectively requires viewing the organization as a total system. Everything is interconnected. In an organization all functions, departments and processes touch and influence one another. The organization is like an organism. Thinking in systems terms facilitates the ability to intervene in one sub-system and have an impact on all other sub-systems.

Capitalize on friction and convert it from negative to positive
Change triggers friction and resistance. To convert these forces from negative barriers to positive enablers begins with acceptance of friction as inevitable.

Employ continuous feedback for learning
The conversion from unhealthy to healthy friction is realized by employing continuous feedback for learning.

Anticipate natural cycles of transformation
To lead organizational transformation effectively entails anticipating the natural cycles of transformation in all systems and addressing the phase of the cycle appropriately; systems evolve through periods of growth, stabilization and standardization, threats of decline and reorganization to meet the challenges.

Discover the few, simple (shared) "rules" that govern the system
While leading organizational change is complex, paradoxically it is essential to discover the few, simple "rules" that govern the system.

Build resilience in the system
Ultimately, leading effective organizational transformation is characterized by building resilience in the system, so future challenges can be addressed quickly and successfully.

Change any one sub-system and have an impact on all other sub-systems.

Sub-systems of an organization exist in a variety of dimensions: human, technological, products/brands, functional (such as HR, Finance, and Manufacturing) or geographical (such as country or region). Awareness of the natural interactions among all subsystems results in bringing people together across boundaries. Left to their own routines, people would otherwise remain within their organizational silos, as if they were not a part of the larger system. That fragmentation carries with it negative, unintended consequences, such as lack of cooperation and inefficiencies.

Example of changing one sub-system and having an impact on all sub-systems from the cases (Section 2)

The need and opportunity to capitalize on the interdependence of sub-systems was central to the initial contract Arri had with Leonard, the new CEO of Greenfields, a regional division of a multinational leader in its industry. This case was introduced in Chapters 2 and 7 and is fully described in Chapter 11.

Greenfields comprised a cluster of businesses in neighboring countries. At their first meeting, Leonard described the challenges facing him and the kind of help he thought he would need from a consultant. He had discovered that indirect cost levels were higher than the average for the parent company, the profit levels relatively low and revenues stagnating or even declining. His initial request to Arri was to do a position analysis aimed at proposing a new organization design which would be more effective and reduce indirect costs.

Arri responded, "Many factors influence indirect costs. I'd like to ask you some questions to understand better what those factors may be." The questions were based on the Genesis Urgent Vision framework. The questions pointed the way for a holistic approach in transforming the organization that would be quite different from Leonard's initial thoughts. He had expected that the consultant would provide expert advice on the new organization design. Instead, as he was to discover progressively, Arri would help facilitate a process of dialogue centered transformation and coach the CEO in leading that process. The approach would be comprehensive and engage management in a co-design process aimed at growing and re-inventing the performance power of the organization from within, including improvement of the cost base.

Arri proceeded with his questions:
"To what extent do people across the organization have the same understanding of the winning business concept? If they don't, then people will work in different directions creating unnecessary costs due to inefficiencies."
"To what extent is the behavior of people supportive of the winning business concept? If they don't, people may be focusing at cross-purposes, also resulting in inefficiencies and increasing costs."
"To what extent is there clarity on the business processes within which people do their work and the decision making authorities at the key steps of the processes? If they don't, the misunderstandings will undoubtedly cause friction, re-work and increasing indirect costs."
"What is the structure of the meetings? Are the meetings adding value? Are the participants those who should attend the meetings? In a regional organization, people must travel distances, usually by air, at considerable cost of money and time. If the meetings are not properly designed and led, then the meetings themselves become a financial and psychic cost."

Leonard responded: "These are all valid questions and we don't have the answers yet. We do have a new regional organization structure that was the decided by my predecessor and imposed on the people without consultation." Jasper, the HR director confirmed: "People don't necessarily understand or accept the new regional organization."

Arri: "An effective way to begin the process to not only reduce costs, but raise the performance of the total organization, is to understand the answers to these questions and build a plan of action based on the findings. We find this is done best when based on the results of a series of interviews to be conducted by the consultant with representatives from all countries, different levels and all functions; perhaps, thirty or so people."

Leonard agreed, contracted with Arri and launched the organizational transformation process. Flexibly and with openness he let go of his own ideas for commencing the organizational development process and embraced an approach that was more comprehensive and more participative and he hoped, most likely, more effective. Leonard and Arri commenced their relationship in the spirit of trust.

As the interviews proceeded, Arri met again with Leonard in the autumn of Year 1 to discuss the initial findings. Leonard greeted Arri with a doubt as to whether to continue with the project, that he had dubbed, "the organizational learning" project. His parent company had purchased a global company in their industry that included operations in the Greenfields region. Leonard would now also need to lead the integration of his division, Greenfields, with Bluefields (a fictitious name for the acquired company's division located in the same region as Greenfields). Leonard appeared stressed and overloaded. In addition, he was already leading several other major projects, including the design and implementation of a new IT system and a large divestiture. He also maintained his priorities to reduce the indirect costs and enhance the performance of the total business. Leonard wondered aloud, that given so many projects that were hitting simultaneously, whether it would be better to put the organizational learning project on hold and tackle the other challenges first. He then excused himself for another commitment and told Arri he would return in two hours to continue the discussion.

In the two hours available to him, Arri thought about Leonard's best approach to deal with his complex and varied challenges; their interdependence appeared striking. Guided by the comprehensive framework of the Genesis Urgent Vision model, he sketched a preliminary integrated approach that would address all the challenges.

Upon his return, Leonard reviewed the schematic proposal and quickly agreed. He immediately saw how the elements fit together and could also be handled in parallel with one another. He was excited by the potential power of the integrated systems approach. He recognized that all of the strategic initiatives were interdependent and if he had approached them sequentially, as he originally intended, the process would undoubtedly have cost far more time, money and effort and no doubt would also have required re-work where different initiatives were potentially not well coordinated. The holistic approach, instead, would most likely create synergies, tight coordination and save time, money and effort. It would also, he hoped and expected, increase the probability of success. With this realization he expressed a new attitude of optimism, energy and confidence. Leonard signed on for a macro process of organizational transformation that he would lead and Arri would facilitate.

Capitalize on friction and convert it from negative to positive

The creation of value in all human systems requires constructive confrontation between and among diverse points of view; i.e., healthy friction. To facilitate this awareness, as we saw in Chapter 5, Discovering healthy friction, Arri introduced his clients to a martial arts exercise and debriefed it with them. Instead of a common avoidance of friction, individuals can learn to be open to challenges of personal knowledge and convictions and challenge others openly, as well.

Teams and organizations innovate and produce results through the healthy friction between the forces of standardization and the forces of creativity, as Arri explains in his book, The Road Within. It is the process of dialogue, both strategic and relational, that transforms potentially destructive friction into healthy friction with creative results.

Example of capitalizing on friction from Genesis cases (Section 2)

Healthy friction was well illustrated in Chapter 13, Accelerated Strategy Development. As introduced above in Chapters 3 and 6, the multi functional team worked on developing its China Growth strategy and in so doing utilized healthy friction in at least two ways. First, the diversity of the team's functions and nationalities assured different perspectives that would need to be integrated. Secondly, the facilitator, Kees, and the project manager had agreed on an agenda design that they anticipated would be met by resistance. Yet, they believed the agenda would be essential in helping the team to achieve the goal of developing the strategy within the limited time of the 3 days of the meeting.

By the afternoon of the first day, the agenda called for subgroups to work on developing solutions. The project leader and Kees had planned that different subgroups would work simultaneously, in parallel, on different, albeit related, topics, e.g., manufacturing, marketing, finance, etc. As they anticipated, the participants raised several objections to the process. The critical juncture of the meeting had arrived. Given the shortness of time in the meeting, some were skeptical that the solutions generated in the sub-groups could ultimately be integrated. They feared that the sub-groups might diverge irreconcilably. In addition, some continued to doubt that the strategy could be successful by focusing only on the top line, tier-one product segment. Next, the amount of time for the exercise, approximately two hours, seemed impossibly short to achieve complex and important outcomes, especially since many were tired due to jet lag. Finally, some felt a need for more guidance and input from senior management.

Kees made sure that all objections were fully raised. First, he guided the group to review MJ's reasoning as to why the focus on top-line, tier-one products was essential. Kees also pointed out that MJ had made the decision and it was no longer negotiable. Kees also explained that given the time limitations for the meeting as established by the sponsors that they had no choice but to take the risk and work in subgroups in parallel on the different yet related topics. There would not have been enough time to work sequentially. Kees also pointed out to the team the progress the team had made to that point in the meeting which provided a base for the proposed exercise to be successful. He pointed out that the team had been working collaboratively during the meeting to that point in spite of their different perspectives.

Next, Kees addressed the objection to having only two hours for the exercise. He explained that while the time would be too short to develop comprehensive plans as elements for the total strategy, that this exercise would be a first iteration and two hours would be sufficient. The participants needed to remember that over the succeeding 90 days there would be time to flesh out the strategy in greater detail. Kees stressed the ground rule of "vigor" rather than "rigor" and the need to confidently tap into the respective knowledge and expertise of every participant in the room. Finally, for those who felt a need for more guidance, there were two draft documents that had been prepared by Kees and the project leader: one for the make or buy strategy and the other for the 5 year sales projections.

While the arguments were persuasive, not every participant was convinced. Ultimately, the project leader needed to invoke his decision making authority and instruct the participants to form the groups around the priority topics. As he later reported to Kees, this moment was frightening. He feared rebellion and needed to muster his courage to be directive. With continued hesitation by some, they all cooperated, or at least, complied. They assigned themselves to the priority solution areas that they had identified earlier, each of which would result in a preliminary plan: HR recruitment, manufacturing facilities, make-buy sourcing, 5 year marketing and sales, engineering intellectual property protection, creation of China as an independent business region within the HMM, Inc. structure, and IT infrastructure.

As the facilitator, Kees moved from group to group to support them in their process of working. He also assured that each group had a moderator and a note taker. He coached them to work quickly, listen to one another and focus on points of agreement.

The next phase of the agenda was entitled, "Joint sharing of draft solutions". The first day of work was concluded with brief reports from each of the subgroups. They had all come over the hump of resistance; clearly, each group had been productive. The day concluded with a sense of accomplishment. Before going to dinner, Kees, the project leader and the subgroup leaders transcribed all the proposals into an edited and consistent format for in-depth review the next morning.

On the morning of the second day the results of day 1 were reviewed. Each of the subgroups presented their draft solutions for their part of the strategic plan in detail to the full group. Each group demonstrated creativity, practicality and consistency with the clear goals set out by the sponsors. Progressively, it dawned upon the group that the China Growth strategic plan had now been fully established in broad strokes! They amazed themselves. Palpable, positive energy swept the group. The previous day's resistance, anxiety and feeling of being on a "mission impossible" flipped to a mood of high motivation and optimism. They also recognized that not only would the China Growth strategy, when implemented, be a boon to HMM, Inc., each individual also stood to gain. It was a career opportunity to be a part of designing and implementing a business of such scale and strategic import for the corporation.

The subgroups reconvened to refine their draft solutions in consideration of what they heard from their colleagues in the other subgroups. The interdependencies of the plans began to be addressed explicitly. They all recognized that the individual plans would need to be further integrated in order to create the final, holistic strategy. The integration would happen in iterations.

After a brief introduction to the action planning process and the overall project time lines by Kees and the project leader, the subgroups convened once again. This time they worked on their 90 day action plans specifying how they would expand and substantiate their initial strategic solutions, as necessary. They also planned points of communication among the sub-groups, with the support of the project leader and Kees. They were confident that after 90 days they would have a fully integrated, robust and powerful China Growth strategic plan.

The action planning culminated in another full group meeting in which each of the individual action plans was shared. The alignment that had pleased everyone in the morning was further reinforced. In addition, they all experienced the creative tension of working efficiently and quickly to prepare the final presentation to the sponsors and the top management teams of HMM and Q&I the next day. The subgroups met one final time to refine their presentations. The full group met one more time to listen to the presentations of each subgroup as a dress rehearsal.

The CEOs of HMM and Q&I and their respective management teams returned to the proceedings. The presentations were presented confidently. All elements of the new strategy were accepted by the leaders and their colleagues with only one exception. MJ required a more thorough analysis as quickly as possible regarding the need to protect their intellectual property in a country famous for intellectual property abuses. Some managers on all levels had expressed doubts of manufacturing in China at all for this reason. MJ recognized that the doubts needed to be thoroughly addressed, both to protect the company, as well as to assure that his managers continued to support the strategy.

The final activity of the conference was a review of the process and progress achieved in the meeting. The sponsors, the team leader and Kees had been the central team in designing and executing every step of the meeting process. They felt pleased with the progress and further committed to a disciplined process over the coming 90 days. The commitment remained high; as did the optimism that the process would yield a winning China Growth strategic plan. The friction experienced across the diverse team, between Kees as the facilitator and the team, as well as between the team and senior management had been healthy—an essential ingredient of the team's productive strategic dialogue.

Employ continuous feedback for learning

All systems are characterized by inputs, throughputs, outputs and feedback loops. Feedback either reinforces and augments inputs or balances and attenuates the inputs. If there is weak capability to give and receive feedback, the system becomes brittle and is more susceptible to breakdown. Effective organizations also have multiple feedback processes, both quantitative and qualitative, from internal as well as external stakeholders. This feedback tracks multiple dimensions that are key to the functioning of the organization, including the customer trends, competition, technology developments, as well as internal system and employee performance, etc. Feedback on the level of the organization and its units is central to the process of strategic dialogue.

Feedback on the level of the individual is central to the process of relational dialogue. Effective individuals solicit, and are open to, feedback from multiple others on the impact of their behavior. This feedback supports learning and helps the individual change behavior to become more effective.

Example of feedback for learning from Genesis cases (Section 2)

The interviews we conduct as consultants at the outset of a transformation process provide the client leadership team with comprehensive feedback on what is working well and what needs to be improved as they embark on their organizational transformation process. At every stage of the transformation process, feedback is employed to monitor progress. During the course of the macro process of transformation over months or even years, we periodically conduct new rounds of interviews in order to update the feedback on how the organization is functioning and how well the transformation is being implemented. During meetings and at the end of meetings, we formally ask participants for feedback on what has worked well and what needs to be improved in the process.

Anticipate natural cycles of transformation

Leading transformation means intervening in and working with the natural cycle of transformation through which all systems progress. This is not a new idea. "Nothing endures but change", Heraclitus is purported to have said in 500 B.C. The panarchy model, created by Gunderson and Holling, describes *Stages of the Adaptive Cycle: Basic Ecosystem Dynamics*, a model which identifies four basic stages of the evolution of ecosystems: exploitation, conservation, release and reorganization. All ecosystems, from the cellular to the global level, including organizations, are seen to go through these four stages of a dynamic adaptive cycle.

The ***exploitation*** stage is one of rapid expansion, such as when an organization finds its niche and grows rapidly.

The *conservation* stage
emphasizes slow accu-
mulation and storage of energy,
material and know how, such
as when the organization
evolves and standardizes in
order to stabilize for a time.

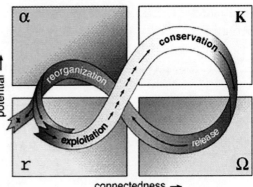

connectedness →

The *release* occurs rapidly,
as when the organization
declines or is threatened to
decline due to competition,
or changed internal conditions.

Reorganization can also occur rapidly, as when an organization makes
significant changes to respond to the phase of release in order to grow
once again.

The panarchy model describes the process as continuous: *reorganization*
evolves once again to *exploitation* and so on.

Example of anticipating natural cycles of transformation from Genesis cases (Section 2)

In the introduction to this chapter, The Leadership Conference served
as an example of how to view the organization as a total system during
a transformation process. The Leadership Conference represented a
culminating event in the macro process of the merger between Euro
Corp and ABC. In Chapter 5 it was introduced as having been made
possible by the moment of shared awareness in the meeting of the new
management team as they designed and agreed the framework for the
new organization.

In this section, the Leadership Conference is viewed from the perspective
that the merger process exemplified the reorganization phase of the
natural cycle of transformation of organizations. The merger had
been triggered by the threats of decline, the release phase, which both
companies had been experiencing; each one had not been large enough
to sustain competition with the larger players in their industry. The
leaders of the merger hoped that the reorganization would lead to new
growth, the exploitation phase of the natural cycle of organizational
transformation.

The Leadership Conference focused on designing the details of the newly merged Euro Corp organization with the top levels of management. It was also intended to mobilize commitment for implementation of the top three-four levels of management of the company.

The Leadership Conference had represented an effort to compress the stages that the model, Stages of the Adaptive Cycle, suggests would unfold "naturally" over time. As a newly merged company, it needed to reorganize. Neither of the prior organizational designs of the two merged entities, the old Euro Corp and ABC were suitable to capitalize on their mutual strengths. They needed a new and more suitable organization design. At the same time, the newly merged company needed to exploit its opportunities to grow its total business rapidly. Brands could be leveraged across new markets and economies of scale could also be optimized. Finally, the newly merged company needed to conserve and leverage its know-how across the entire company so that the merger did not damage the strengths that the prior organizations had developed over the years. The Leadership Conference and the overall transformation process had represented a series of interventions to accelerate the "natural cycle of transformation."

Discover the few, simple (shared) "rules" which govern the system

While we think of systems as complex, research from complexity theory is revealing that complex systems are governed by a limited number of simple rules. Though social ecological systems are affected by many variables, they are usually driven by only a handful of key controlling (often slow-moving) variables (e.g., the buildup of CO_2 in the atmosphere deriving from our fossil fuel economy is a major contributor to climate change). In 1989, Jack Welch, Chairman of GE, famously launched the culture change and productivity improvement process, Workout! with three simple rules: speed, simplicity and self confidence. The process was implemented globally with his personal support and adequate budget. The resultant productivity improvements are legendary in the world of business.

A former client in a merger integration process, the CEO of a Scandinavian transport company employed this principle and expressed it in the following way: "Employees are best motivated by simple messages.

Each year we have one priority which we ask everyone to focus on, e.g., cleanliness or answering every customer's every question, especially in our shops and restaurants." He grew the company successfully year by year during his tenure with consistently high employee morale.

The Genesis Consultative Consensus decision making model (Chapter 2, above) is another example of how a few simple shared rules can positively influence a large, complex organization. All of our cases employed the model as the decision making to support strategic dialogue. Uniformly and consistently, with numerous clients over the years, the model has been embraced. The model simply resolves the dilemma which many leaders experience: how to mobilize commitment through collaboration while retaining decision making authority? The model proposes that the team proceeds with healthy debate until there is consensus in order to mobilize commitment through collaboration; further, it proposes that the ultimate decision, with the consensus or not, is retained by the leader. As our clients report to us, the adoption of the model frequently cures some of the chronic ills of decision making which they have experienced in their cultures over the years, such as "the debate begins after the meeting where the decision was made." That phenomenon is all too frequent and represents a symptom of poor dialogue and either unclear or abruptly unilateral decision making.

Example of discovering the few, simple (shared) "rules" which govern the system from Genesis cases

As an example, early on in a transformation process, I was facilitating a meeting of a CEO and his leadership team. The CEO and the team had already accepted that we would employ the Consultative Consensus model of decision making. As the meeting unfolded an issue arose which generated some heated discussion. The CEO entered the fray with a strong statement. I asked him on the spot, "Is that your opinion, or your decision?" He hesitated, looked surprised and answered, "My opinion." In that moment, he reinforced the Consultative Consensus model. During the healthy debate, he wanted to be a participant and in so doing reserve his decision until after he saw the consensus emerge. His subordinates in the meeting also recognized that during the process of the meeting, before a decision was taken, expressing honest disagreement with the boss was not only acceptable but expected. Later, once the debate had run its course and consensus was evident, the CEO, did, indeed, make the ultimate decision.

Build resilience in the system

Leaders with a systems perspective recognize that results may be ephemeral and do not define identity. Results may go up and down. The more resilient organizations address downturns in results by assessing the reasons why and taking fast, appropriate, dynamic and adaptive action. Most dramatically, the business might actually change its business model, including fundamental aspects of the kinds of products and services that it offers. The resilient organization has the capability to read its compelling needs and opportunities continually. It explores where thresholds exist by engaging in dialogue and healthy debate both internally and with external stakeholders. Resilience is a virtuous circle: dialogue (with others or with oneself when in a perilous situation) facilitates shared awareness, engenders trust and counters fear. To adapt quickly and appropriately to changes in the environment, resilient organizations invest in making their business models, strategies, cultures, processes and organization designs more resilient through the development of continuous feedback loops.

Resilience of natural systems, write Walker and Salt, "…means the ability of the system to withstand disturbance and maintain or adapt its state is the key to sustainability of the system". "A (natural) system's resilience can be measured by its distance from … thresholds. The closer you are to a threshold, the less it takes to be pushed over." Resilience … "is all about knowing if and where thresholds exist and having the capacity to manage the system in relation to these thresholds."

"Sustainable development is not sustainable in our world today. We need to build resilience in systems where we can," states Gene Likens, world renowned eco-scientist.

(Human) resilience is " . . . the process of adapting well in the face of adversity, trauma, tragedy, threats or even significant sources of stress . . .", as Parens, Blum and Akhtar posit.

In human systems, (i.e., the individual, the team, the organization or the network) resilience may be thought of as having both "static" as well as "dynamic adaptive" dimensions. The static dimension of resilience relates to maintaining the integrity of the system over time. Companies which lead their industries over time have all maintained their core values, mission and/or vision of what they have represented since their creation. They have maintained their integrity. Their identity endures, as Collins and Porras document in their bestseller, <u>Built to Last</u>.

Example of helping build resilience in the system from Genesis cases (Section 2)

The mandate to globalize the Purchasing Organization of MNX, followed by six years of integration activities (as discussed in Chapters 1, 4, 5 and 12) were all disturbances to the status quo. Instead of those disturbances being met with resistant behaviors and failure, the transformation process supported the individual managers and their new teams to work through their resistance and respond resiliently. As the various teams gained experience in working together, their sense of mutual accountability, trust and support for one another grew, which further enhanced their resilience.

One example is found at the turning point when the Global Purchasing Leadership Team gelled as a team. One of the members, whom we shall call Luigi, reported that his regional boss privately had been instructing him to focus only on regional priorities and ignore the global priorities of the Global Purchasing Leadership Team. Luigi asked his global purchasing colleagues for help on how to manage his regional boss, pursue the global priorities and keep his job. Over time, he succeeded on all counts. Luigi demonstrated resilience in the face of pressure from his regional boss by getting support from colleagues. The Global Purchasing Leadership Team represented resilience, in turn, by supporting him to overcome the opposition from his regional boss.

Lessons in transforming the entire system

Organizational transformation is enhanced by systems thinking.

Every change, whether it is strategic, cultural, structural or in business processes, that might be in one region, department or product arena, will have an impact on the total organization. Deliberate change in one sub-system will impact on all other sub-systems.

Systems naturally manifest friction, i.e., conflict. The negative energy can be converted to positive energy through dialogue.

Effective systems are based on feedback and continually self-correct and adapt. Feedback on behavior and decisions, a key form of dialogue, supports learning, change, and a culture whereby these values become self reinforcing.

Organizations evolve through natural cycles. Awareness of this helps in guiding the change process. For example, there is a phase when standardization is important after a period of significant growth; and there is also a phase to make significant changes when decline is threatened.

Awareness of and working with the natural cycles supports the resilience of the organization.

The first opportunity to view the organization with a systems perspective is during the initial contracting between the facilitator and the client. The facilitator should resist the temptation to accept the client's common narrow and fragmented approach to organizational transformation. The argument is based on the understanding that to improve performance and results requires a holistic approach grounded in the view that the organization is a complex system. The leader and the leadership team can be supported to design and implement a macro process that addresses the organization as a complex system.

Chapter 9
Discovery: Action Learning

"I've been CEO for one year now. I was hired from within. All of us on the management team have worked with one another for years. We know each other well. We are stuck in the cultural habits of how we relate to one another, based on our prior roles and the patterns that form over time. I believe we need to change our behavior (based on emotional awareness to create more energy and creativity). This is the priority of the organizational and leadership development work which we want to do with you," my new client explained in our first detailed interview.

With this objective in mind, I proceeded with interviewing the other members of the management team, representative board members and representative staff. The CEO and I met and discussed my write-up of the interview findings.

"I am stunned that there is considerable confusion and disagreement in our management team and in the organization concerning one of our strategic thrusts concerning our leadership in the market. It was already decided by our Board and is in our published strategic plan, so it is disconcerting to discover now, after so much time, that this kind of feeling exists. Is it resistance? What is it?"

The CEO and I continued to review the interview data which showed that this case was not an isolated event. There emerged a consistent pattern that on this and other important issues, "healthy debate and healthy friction" were not well developed in this organization. Important strategic decisions were confused and manifested lack of agreement and weak commitment.

The interview data also revealed the strengths of their culture, as they saw it themselves: collegiality, professionalism, mutual respect, kindness and caring for others. The culture's strengths apparently carried a cost: conflict avoidance and impaired decision making. The CEO and

I then proceeded to design the agenda for a management team meeting based on the interview data and the objective she had set for our work together.

At the beginning of the meeting several members of the team were distressed by the interview feedback. First, while there were many examples of a culture of avoidance, they felt that in their own experience some difficult issues were well addressed. Secondly, while there was feedback that was strongly critical of the management team taking on more work than the organization could comfortably handle, several management team members felt hurt and angry. In a time of budget cuts and economic downturn, of course, people should be expected to work harder, they said.

With determination they wanted immediately to continue to explore the critical feedback and look for solutions. Instead, as the CEO and I had prepared in the agenda, we challenged the team first to re-assert the strengths in their organization and culture. Focusing on this was inspired by the Gestalt (GISC) approach: create positive energy at the outset as a secure emotional basis for subsequently addressing areas "in need of development". The team agreed. The members began to reel off the strengths of the organization and its culture while the CEO recorded them on a flip chart. The list included at least ten items. The CEO reinforced points by changing the black marker to red. The team became emotionally lighter, energetic and positive.

I felt that the CEO had effectively taken on my role as the facilitator at this juncture and I was delighted. In our Genesis way of working we do support our clients to adopt the process skills of facilitation. It seemed to me that by scribing and reinforcing the strengths of the organization as contributed by her colleagues, she manifested positive leadership and inspired her colleagues.

Next, I introduced some concepts and exercises which are integral to dialogue, including the importance of emotions in the decision making process, the idea that perception is reality, and the Genesis Consultative Consensus decision making model. One of the exercises was a series of bilateral dialogues. The partners could discuss anything so long as it was a suggestion or constructive criticism, which heretofore had been unspoken. In an interchange one member offered a constructive critique of a new initiative undertaken by a colleague. I fed back to the team what I saw had occurred and observed that according to the interviews, until this moment, it had been rare that any member of the team would venture constructive criticism of a fellow member or across departmental boundaries. Several team members mentioned that this was new for them and that that kind of behavior should continue to be encouraged.

At this meeting, the management team also agreed to a follow-up meeting including next level managers. They decided to explore fully and debate as necessary the topic about the confusion and disagreement surrounding the strategic thrust of leadership in the market which had arisen in the interviews and had stunned the CEO. They wanted to practice healthy debate and strategic dialogue and do so with a topic of importance to the organization. They also wanted to take the output of the next meeting and use it as input to a process that would culminate some months later in a detailed recommendation from the CEO to the Board.

The CEO asked me to facilitate that next meeting so that she could participate in the dialogue. I strove to role model active facilitation; I asked individuals questions to draw them in and asked others follow-up questions to draw out their meaning. When there appeared to be disagreements, I spotlighted the differences of opinion and checked with the team to be sure the different viewpoints were fully expressed. The meeting fulfilled their expectations. The energy was high, everyone in the meeting contributed openly and disagreements were freely expressed.

A few weeks later, several management team members reported to me proudly that at one of their regular management team meetings, they had taken on a sensitive issue in an unusually open way; important disagreements had been freely expressed. The topic concerned whether or not to add a staff member to one department. Well before the management team meeting, the VP of the department in question had already secured an agreement in principle from the CEO to add the staff member. Instead of formalizing the decision, the CEO decided to take the question to the full management team. She wanted the team's commitment to the decision. This was new behavior.

At the management team meeting, several members challenged the proposal. This was new behavior, too. The team pointed out that adding even a critical staff member at this time would hurt staff morale since everyone knew that the CEO and the management team had already imposed tight policies due to budget cuts, including a hiring freeze, pay rise freeze and several layoffs. The CEO agreed with the consensus and did not sign off on the additional staff member.

I felt excited and proud that the management team had made progress on openly discussing difficult disagreements and it was without my facilitation. I took this as a sign of their action learning.

I was also experiencing action learning. I had begun this assignment after more than a year of Gestalt study and training. I had been more explicit with these clients than many other clients in the past through a meeting on the role emotions play in decision making and relationships. I was evolving my style as an organizational consultant from my earlier period of focusing principally on employing strategic dialogue to now focusing on both the strategic and the relational dimensions, with greater emphasis than ever on the relational and the emotional sides of leadership behavior. I was learning through my own new, experimental actions as a consultant.

Action learning

Change is learning and learning is change.

Action learning entails:

- receiving feedback on one's own behavior and/or on the situation the team or organization is facing
- becoming aware of one's emotions and the most effective response—the behaviors to let go and new behaviors with which to experiment
- mobilizing the energy to try out the new behavior
- acting out new strategies and behaviors
- completing the action
- reflecting on one's experience and distilling learning
- repeating the cycle with an emphasis on practicing the new strategies and behaviors which are useful

Action learning is enabled by trusting relationships. It is analogous to the Gestalt cycle of experience which emphasizes the process of progressing from awareness to mobilized energy to action to completion and making meaning of the entire cycle.

The management team received feedback through the interview process and through the individual coaching sessions that I held with each member of the team. They became aware that their culture of mutual respect, professionalism and collegiality carried the cost of conflict avoidance and incomplete decision making on some important strategic questions. In their first meeting they felt their energy to experiment with new behaviors. The feedback bothered them. They wanted to do something about it. Several were eager to engage more fully in healthy debate and that was new behavior in the culture. The ideas I shared with them, particularly regarding the role of emotions in decision making, etc. was found especially helpful by several members. In the exercises, they took some risks by giving a colleague constructive criticism. This contributed to the trust already present in the team and built on it.

The second meeting was an opportunity to practice healthy debate and dialogue while addressing a real problem. A priority strategic thrust, decided upon earlier, had left some members of the organization confused and with little commitment to its implementation. They made progress with both objectives.

Spontaneously, the management team, without the presence of the consultant, myself, practiced healthy debate further on their own. They challenged their own CEO on the decision of whether or not to make an exception to existing policy and make a new hire. After the constructive challenge to the CEO, the team and the CEO chose not to make an exception to the existing policy. The team trusted one another enough to take the risk of the healthy debate on this decision. In so doing they contributed to deepening trust among themselves.

This management team was learning new behaviors by practicing them. The motivation and energy to learn the new behaviors was stimulated by the interview feedback and the introduction to the concepts, methods and potential benefits of healthy debate. The feedback had catalyzed shared awareness of a side of their culture which would be beneficial to develop further. It was the shared awareness that triggered the motivation and energy to learn through practice of new behaviors.

Organizational transformation to raise the performance of the organization at its core depends on individuals, initially and especially, the leaders, to change their behavior. This action learning process is embedded in the process of dialogue, both strategic and relational.

Example of action learning from Genesis cases (Section 2)

Action learning as integral to organizational transformation at each stage of the process was exemplified in the Chapter 14 case, Merger Integration. Through the series of preparatory Leadership Team meetings and including the Leadership Conference itself, the managers did the design work themselves; they made the decisions. This was the action component. At the same time they applied tools for dialogue and organizational design that I provided as the facilitator and they reflected on how effective they were in using the tools. This was the learning component.

By their own assessment they made significant progress. At the end of the first Leadership Team meeting, the participants summarized their work:

"As we continue with the merger integration and transformation process of the new Euro Corp., we have made the Euro Corp. (organization structure) matrix workable by defining the key processes and clarifying the roles and responsibilities within the leadership team. We also deepened our teamwork. This has been the next decisive step of the integration process."

At the end of the second Leadership Team meeting, the participants summarized their work again: "We have also deepened our trusting relationships with one another."

Lessons in action learning

Organizational transformation is an action learning process, for all concerned, the leader, the facilitator and the members of the organization.

As facilitators and leaders open themselves to feedback on their own behavior and make appropriate changes, they become role models and others will be positively influenced by their example.

Learning to change behavior requires patience, risk taking and building of trust.

By employing the principles of trust building, mobilizing commitment and strategic and relational dialogue, clients will experience new behaviors that they and their colleagues employ. The facilitator can help clients reflect on those experiences, make meaning from them and learn to incorporate these behaviors in their leadership styles by providing feedback in team meetings and through coaching individuals.

Chapter 10
Summary: Principles and Methods for
Leading Organizational Transformation

Organizational transformation must encompass the entire system. To address less than the entire system would produce unintended consequences for the whole system since all sub-systems are interconnected for optimal impact.

The facilitator supports the transformation process by facilitating moments of shared awareness, meetings of strategic and relational dialogue and macro processes of mobilizing commitment across the entire organization.

The foundation of transformation is created through the development of trusting relationships. The building of trust is enabled through relational dialogue which entails two-way feedback between individuals on their behavior. Through feedback they discover the emotional and substantive impact they have had on one another. They also learn to change their behavior in order to have the impact which they intend to have. Relational dialogue enables strategic dialogue, the means for making sound decisions which are implemented and produce results.

Different perceptions and their associated different realities may be barriers and are openly addressed in the search for shared understanding; diversity becomes a source of strength.

The boundaries for each meeting are designed according to the principle of freedom within a framework. The boundaries provide coherence for what is addressed and decided in each meeting and how all meetings complement one another.

The meetings aim for multiplier affects: the leveraging of total resources and the strengthening of individual capability and performance across the entire organization.

Throughout the journey of organizational transformation new ideas are crystallized through shared awareness which in turn catalyzes mobilized commitment for implementation of new behavior—a synergistic process of dialogue and action learning.

Section 2
Cases of Organizational Transformation

Facilitating the Macro Process which mobilizes commitment

Facilitating the Meeting which employs dialogue

Chapter 11
Long-term Improvement
Facilitating a macro process which mobilizes commitment

Introduction
This comprehensive 4 year process of organizational transformation and development engaged multiple levels of the organization, beginning with the leadership team. It began as a merger-integration and evolved into a continuous transformation process of organizational development and improvement. Over the four years, the transformation process progressed consistently and effectively through the tenures of two CEOs. Each CEO, in turn, led the transformation process by employing the complete Genesis change process by mobilizing commitment to craft the Urgent Vision, set transformation priorities, launch teams/ work with teams and align behaviors. It also evolved into increasing engagement by the top management teams in constructively learning how to adapt their behaviors. This involved employing relational dialogue, in order to have the impact intended to implement the operating framework and deliver the business results.

Chronology of the macro process	
Launching the project: contracting between the client CEO, SVP HR and Genesis Consulting Group partner, consultant Arri Pauw	August, Year 1
Mobilizing the organization; Addressing uncertainty/ building shared understanding; Leadership Conference I	October, Year 1
Kick-starting the merger integration; The new Senior Management Team Meeting I	December, Year 1
Enlisting the wider organization; Validating and Implementing the Operating Framework with teams led by each Senior Management Team member	
e.g., Country Retail Teams	February Year 2

e.g., Interface Meeting: Region Y (corporate) Marketing and Country Retail Organizations	March Year 2
Maintaining momentum; Senior Management Team Meeting II	March, Year 2
A new beginning; the CEO resigns for personal reasons and is replaced by a new CEO The new CEO contracts with the Genesis consultant, Arri Pauw to continue supporting the implementation of the new organization	August Year 2
Mobilizing the organization—the next round of interviews and Leadership Conference II	November Year 2
Establishing how to lead by example; Senior Management Team Meeting III	February Year 3
Building bridges; Multinational X/ Region Y Marketing Meeting—September Year 3	
Mobilizing the Organization; Leadership Conference III—Individuality and Interdependency	November Year 3
Building leadership effectiveness; Coaching of Senior Management Team Members	Year 4-Year 5
Continuing to strengthen the top team; Senior Management Team Meeting IV	March Year 4

Launching the project: contracting between the client CEO, SVP HR and the Genesis Consulting Group partner, consultant Arri Pauw

A new CEO, Leonard (a fictitious name) had just taken the position to head Greenfields (another fictitious name), a regional division of a multinational leader in its industry. Greenfields comprised a cluster of neighboring countries. He was looking for consulting assistance in developing his organization. His boss suggested Arri Pauw, Genesis Consulting Group with whom the boss had worked on a prior project. Leonard, his HR VP, Jasper, and Arri met for the first time at the end of August, Year 1.

Leonard described the challenges facing him and the kind of help he thought he would need from a consultant. He found indirect cost levels higher than the average for the parent company and profit levels low and revenues stagnating or even declining. His initial request to Arri was to do a position analysis aimed at understanding which positions were necessary and which not and to propose a new organization design which would be more effective and efficient and reduce indirect costs.

Arri responded, "Many factors influence indirect costs. I'd like to ask you some questions to understand better what those factors may be." The questions were based on the Genesis Urgent Vision framework for developing an organization. These questions began to shift the frame for Leonard with an alternative, holistic, systems mental model for understanding and developing the organization. The questions also pointed the way for a means of transforming the organization which would be quite different from Leonard's initial approach. He had expected that the consultant would provide expert advice on the new organization design. Instead, as he was to discover progressively, the consultant would help facilitate a process of transformation and coach the CEO in so doing. The approach would be comprehensive and engage the organization in a co-design process aimed at growing and re-inventing the performance power of the organization from within, including improvement of the cost base.

Arri proceeded with his questions.
"To what extent do people across the organization have the same understanding of the winning business concept? If they don't, then people will work in different directions creating unnecessary costs due to inefficiencies."
"To what extent is the behavior of people supportive of the winning business concept? If they don't, people may be focusing at cross-purposes, also resulting in inefficiencies and increasing costs."
"To what extent is there clarity on the business processes within which people do their work and the decision making authorities at the key steps of the processes? If they don't, the misunderstandings will undoubtedly cause friction, re-work and increasing indirect costs."

"What is the meeting structure? Are the meetings adding value? Are the participants those who should be in the meetings? In a regional organization, people must travel distances, usually by air, at considerable cost of money and time. If the meetings are not properly designed and run the meetings themselves become a financial and psychic cost."

Leonard responded: "These are all valid questions and we don't have the answers yet. We do have a new regional organization structure which was the decided by my predecessor and imposed on the people without consultation." Jasper, the HR director confirmed: "People don't necessarily understand or accept the new regional organization."

Arri: "An effective way to begin the process of not only reducing costs, but aiming toward raising the performance of the total organization, is to understand the answers to these questions and build a plan of action based on the findings. We find this is best done through a series of interviews to be conducted by the consultant with representatives from all countries, different levels and all functions; perhaps, thirty or so people."

Leonard agreed and launched the organizational transformation process. In so doing he demonstrated flexibility and openness to new ways of thinking. He was ready to replace his ideas for commencing the organizational development process with new ideas which sounded more comprehensive, more involving of the people in the organization and hopefully, more effective. The relationship between Leonard and Arri commenced in the spirit of trust.

As the interviews proceeded, Arri met again with Leonard in the autumn, Year 1 to discuss the initial findings. Leonard greeted Arri with a doubt as to whether to continue with the project, which he had dubbed, "the organizational learning" project. His parent company had purchased a global company in their industry, which included operations in the Greenfields region. Leonard would now also need to lead the integration of his division, Greenfields, with Bluefields (a fictitious name for the acquired company's division located in the same region as Greenfields). Leonard appeared stressed and overloaded. In addition, he was already leading several other major projects—the design and implementation of a new IT system and a large divestiture. He also continued his intention to reduce the indirect costs and enhance the performance of the total business. Leonard wondered aloud, that given so many projects which were hitting simultaneously, whether it would be better to put the organizational learning project on hold and tackle the other challenges first. He then excused himself for another commitment and told Arri he would return in two hours to continue the discussion.

In the two hours available to him, Arri thought about the best approach for Leonard to deal with his complex and varied challenges; their interdependence appeared striking. Consequently, he sketched a preliminary integrated approach which would address all the challenges, guided by the comprehensive framework of the Genesis Urgent Vision model and Genesis Transformation approach. Upon his return, Leonard reviewed the schematic proposal and heartily agreed. He immediately saw how the elements fit together and could also be handled in parallel with one another. He quickly grasped the potential power of the integrated approach. He recognized that all of the strategic initiatives were interdependent and if he had approached them sequentially, as he originally intended, the process would undoubtedly have cost far more time, money and effort; no doubt it would also have required re-work where different initiatives were potentially not well coordinated. The holistic approach would most likely create synergies, tight coordination and save time, money and effort. With this realization he expressed a new attitude of optimism, energy and confidence. Leonard signed on for a macro process of organizational transformation that he would lead and Arri would facilitate.

"The Merger Process of Greenfields and Bluefields"
It began by establishing guiding principles against which to evaluate every step of the process.
Clarity in the market—not disturbing relationships with customers and consumers
Clarity for the people—giving them security and self-confidence
Clarity of Leadership—in direction and decision making

The approach also listed the givens in the process which needed to be taken into account at every step going forward:

The timeframe for the merger as determined by the Leonard's superiors, including the divestiture that needed to be made

The requirements of the parent company for organization design

The timeframe for the implementation of the new IT system

The findings of an organization study of Greenfields which had recently been completed

The best practices of Bluefields

The approach also identified the key business processes to be managed both independently and interdependently which would be instrumental to the success of the merger:

Performance Management process

Divestiture process

Appointment process for the top two levels of the new organization

Organization design process, including the definition of the macro process steps and decision making authorities

The IT process, including the phases of implementation

People transfer process

Next, the approach proposed a series of steps to redesign the organization into the newly merged entity, with ambitious deadlines:

By 15th October:

There would be one CEO, Leonard, for both companies in the merger and he would lead each of the existing Senior Management Teams in achieving the Year 1 results

By mid/end November:

A new, single Senior Management Team for the merged entity would be appointed and take responsibility for:

Jointly agreeing and taking ownership for the overall merger process

Defining the macro steps of the key business processes and the associated high level decision making authorities

By 1st January, Year 2

The new Senior Management Team would take full ownership for delivering the Year 2 results of both Greenfields and Bluefields.

The new Senior Management Team would implement the merger, including the divestiture process

Senior Management Team members who led a business process would lead multifunctional/multinational teams with people from Greenfields and Bluefields to design the more detailed key process steps and decision making authorities within and between processes
By 1st April
The results of the business process work would be reviewed and approved by the Senior Management Team
The Senior Management Team members would lead the work on redesigning their departments (the roles and the appointments) consistent with all prior work
By 1st of May
The results of the organization design work would be approved by the Senior Management Team
Announcements of results would be shared with individual employees
The Divestiture process
Steps in the process for an individual
Someone is being offered a job in the company to be disposed
If yes, no problem, he/she goes
If no: he/she stays in Greenfields
It needs to be agreed with the unions what the process/outcome is of selecting people, offering them a position and what to do when they refuse the offered position. Key principles:
Selected people will be offered a position in the organization of the disposed company (see below how to get there)
If they refuse they can stay with Greenfields
Then new people can be recruited (from outside) into the disposed company
Later, the merger of Bluefields and Greenfields will take place

Mobilizing the organization: addressing uncertainty/ building shared understanding;
Leadership Conference I—October, Year 1

Leonard was receiving more and more questions about the next steps in the merger. People were concerned about their personal futures, when decisions would be taken and what the new organization would look like. To address these questions and anxieties, Leonard agreed to hold the first Leadership Conference with the top four levels of the organization. The purpose would be three-fold: first, to reinforce the business targets for the coming year (Year 2) and the necessity to achieve them; secondly, to validate the output from the interviews Arri had conducted and to further identify any other organizational barriers to performance; thirdly, to inform the people on the planned key steps to integrate the merger with Bluefields. Approximately 150 members of Greenfields were invited. The top levels of management of the newly acquired Bluefields organization would be invited to a separate conference, with the same objectives, in the near future once the merger process was designed and underway.

Leonard opened the conference with an overview. As input for the section of the conference regarding organization, Arri presented a synthesis of the interviews. Next, sub-groups were given ample time to validate and/or amend the interview findings and report their conclusions back to the full plenary. The conclusions resulted in a set of recommendations which would prove essential in designing the next steps of the organizational change process and the broad areas of focus that Leonard wanted his organization to achieve during this moment of turbulent, complex change.

The day concluded with a one hour presentation from Leonard in which he summarized key conclusions from the day, the macro steps and timing of the merger process going forward and the key steps of the process of appointments to the new organization. All now knew by when their anxious uncertainty would be alleviated and their key questions would be answered: "Do I have a job? If so, what is it?" Leonard also announced that no later than the beginning of December, Year 1, he would appoint the members of his new senior management team.

The macro steps reinforced the same principles which Leonard embraced with which to guide the change process. Delivering results were dependent upon:
Clarity in the market—not disturbing relationships with customers and consumers
Clarity for the people—giving them security and self-confidence
Clarity of Leadership—in direction and decision making

This meeting was an early step in building shared understanding that would ultimately result, later, in the formulation of the Urgent Vision of the new Greenfields organization. The meeting also was an early turning point in improving the relative level of comfort of the people with the merger.

Being informed and having been able to give input began to ameliorate the anxiety of the unknown consequences of the merger. Most everyone felt heard and involved in the change process. Overall, the attendees felt positive. The culture of dialogue had been introduced.

The meeting was also a platform for Leonard to communicate and further consolidate his leadership. Through the meeting design, his words and his choice of consultant, it was clear to all that Leonard cultivated feedback and listening and was committed to continue to involve a wide number of people from both companies across the geographies and functions in determining the details of the new organization design. He also provided clear direction on the transformation processes which would unfold; and he unambiguously reinforced the importance of focusing on and delivering business results.

Leonard and Arri shared with each other that they both felt that the meeting had been successful in creating positive energy and a sense of optimism among the participants on the next steps of the merger integration/organizational transformation process.

Next, preparations began for the similar conference to be held with the top levels of management of the new acquisition, Bluefields. Once again, the conference would be preceded by a round of interviews to be conducted by Arri. The meeting would be a half day in early November. And while it would be briefer, it would serve to send similar messages to the Bluefields community as Leonard had provided to his Greenfields colleagues.

Based on all he had learned from the process thus far, Leonard next designed the structure of the new organization, beginning with the positions in The Senior Management Team. He next planned to have a meeting in December with the members of the new Senior Management Team to launch the new organization with Arri as the facilitator.

Kick-starting the merger integration;
The new Senior Management Team Meeting I—December, Year 1

Leonard knew that it would be required to have the agreement of his boss regarding the new structure before convening his new leadership team, the Senior Management Team, for the December meeting. Until this point, The Leonard's superiors had regarded Greenfields as one country, rather than a region, with a cluster of countries. Consequently, they had not wanted to establish country managers, which they considered an unnecessary extra layer and extra cost. To the contrary, Leonard felt that country managers would be essential to maximize performance in local markets, given the differences in customer needs and consumer tastes from one Greenfields country to another. Without much persuasion necessary, the boss readily agreed. The road was clear for the launch of the new Greenfields Senior Management Team.

The December meeting to launch the new Senior Management Team had three objectives. First, this new team needed to prepare themselves to lead the full integration of the Greenfields/Bluefields business across the region while delivering the annual business targets. Second, to achieve this, they had to make a kick-start in operating as team, a special challenge since only some of the members knew each other! Third, to strengthen team functioning, the relationships between and among the top ten leaders of this business would also need development. With such an ambitious agenda, Leonard agreed to make it a three day meeting. The rhythm of the meeting was to alternate the work on the organization design with work on the functioning of the team, including deeper work on strengthening relationships. The agenda was again framed by the Genesis Urgent Vision Model.

Much of content of the Urgent Vision model was found in a model operating framework which Arri had helped develop in prior organizational transformation projects with Greenfields' parent company. The Senior Management Team did not have to "reinvent the wheel", instead they simply had to review, modify as needed and validate the existing operating framework. The agenda focused on seeking agreement on key elements of the newly merged organization: the winning business concept (including targets for the following year); the culture, values and behavior expected (including how the Senior Management team would role model the values and take decisions); the key business processes (including interfaces and the formal meetings to convene); the emerging organization design of the next levels of the organization (including the appointment process for the next levels). The meeting would conclude with next steps to guide the merger process.

In addition to the aim of seeking understanding, buy-in and commitment to the new Operating Framework, the meeting also aimed to accelerate the building of trusting relationships in the Senior Management Team. To this end, Arri organized a structured singing exercise at the end of the first day of work. With a professional singing teacher who also had considerable experience in working with organizations with humor and careful attention to the uniqueness of each client group, the Senior Management Team devoted three hours to singing—individually and in pairs in front of the peers and also as a full group. The feedback from the Senior Management Team was unanimous appreciation for the experience. People reported a strengthened sense of bonding with one another.

In Arri's words, "All the emotions in a team were lived in three hours. People had to expose themselves in their vulnerability, strength, individuality, togetherness, fear and joy in the moment. In the experienced hands of the singing teacher, the Senior Management Team felt safe throughout and gained considerable energy as a team. In three days the Senior Management Team intensively lived the leadership of the business, working together as a team (talking about it and doing it) and gluing relationships between individuals."

At the end of the meeting, evaluating the three days, there was a wide appreciation for what was accomplished. Although most Senior Management Team members were new to the task, all reported that they felt ready, informed, well equipped and energized to take on the challenge. They also reported enthusiasm to work together as a Senior Management Team.

In terms of the Genesis Transformation Model, the Senior Management Team meeting represented the phase of confirming the "Urgent Vision", i.e., their "Operating framework". Simultaneously, the meeting enhanced trust among the members of the Senior Management Team. In the next steps of the process, the organization would work even more explicitly on aligning behaviors to fulfill the agreed vision of the Operating Framework.

Enlisting the wider organization;
Validating and Implementing the Operating Framework with teams
led by each Senior Management Team member

At the conclusion of the December Year 1 meeting, the Senior Management Team agreed to launch the new organization during February and March Year 2. First, each Senior Management Team member would lead a meeting to launch his/her own team by agreeing their purpose, ways of working and decision making authorities while further building the relationships within the team. In addition, they would validate the work on the Operating Framework done to date by the Senior Management Team and tailor it to the unique needs of their own team and department. Secondly, the Senior Management Team members would lead interface meetings between units who shared work in key processes and where the need for clarity in roles and decision making authorities was high. These interface meetings would also focus on correcting dysfunctional behavior. For consistency, all of the meetings were facilitated by Arri.

A second Senior Management Team Meeting was planned to follow these meetings in order to validate the progress of the integration agenda and to review and continue to enhance the functioning of the Senior Management Team.

Examples of Meetings

Country Retail Teams— . . . February Year 2
The first meeting in the sequence brought together the management teams of the three country retail organizations, each headed by a country head who served as a member of the Regional Senior Management Team.

Greenfields
Country Retail Teams
Workshop
... Feb 2001

Purpose:
- Energising the Country Retail teams to assume
collective and individual leadership for the Retail business in Greenfields
- In this context the workshop aims to create amongst the Country Retail teams:
    - ✓ An understanding of the unique added value of the new merged organization and retail in particular
    - ✓ Agreement and commitment regarding the way-we-work as Country Retail, i.e.:
        - o How do we work as Retail business in a country— decision-making authorities within our roles, between our roles, style of leadership and of working together? Including:
        - o How do we work as teams—incl. practical issues, like: agenda, frequency
    - ✓ What is common across the Greenfields Regionand what is unique per country and why and how do we organise for that
    - ✓ How do we work as Retail business with our colleagues—activities and decision making authorities vs other functions
    - ✓ What are the critical steps in the roadmap of the Retail merger process, what is common / unique per country
    - ✓ As a background to all of this, exchange and understand:
        - o The Operating Framework (from the Board Workshop)
        - o The structure of the parent Multinational organization

---

An impasse occurred during these discussions during a debate of what would be the same and what would be different organizationally among the three country organizations. The implicit assumption going in to the meeting was that the structures and ways of working among the countries should be uniform to ease interfaces with corporate functions and standardize processes in order to make them more efficient. As the discussion ensued the participants evinced more and more passion regarding their belief that their customer requirements were different from country to country and so their organizations would need to be different, as well, to accommodate those market differences.

The breakthrough occurred through reference to the Guiding Principle which the Senior Management Team had defined earlier: "growth is in the market". They also considered the Genesis principle of organization transformation, "freedom within the framework". As a consequence, the participants agreed to design their internal roles and their external market interface roles with different perspectives. They would align their key internal roles consistently across all countries for consistency and simplicity in interfacing with corporate functions. At the same time, they agreed that they would allow their external roles, sales and trade marketing, to be different in each country, as appropriate, in order to fit their unique external local market interfaces.

Interface Meeting: Greenfields Central Marketing and Country Retail Organizations— . . . March Year 2

Perhaps the interface with the most negative history was the one between Greenfields Central Marketing and the Country Retail Organizations. Greenfields Central Marketing had been seen by the Country Retail Organizations as micro-managing, continually asking for information and interfering with the Country Retail Organizations while adding hardly any value. The Country Retail Organizations had been seen by Greenfields Central Marketing as "their employees" to be directed.

The meeting entailed debate and agreement on the roles and decision making authorities in marketing between the two organizations. The resulting clarity eliminated a primary cause of friction. The dialogue also focused on building trusting relationships. Each member was invited to make personal commitments to the whole group, as they had a year earlier, as to how they would specifically contribute to making the interface work well in the future.

As the final activity for the meeting, a martial arts teacher who was also a psychologist led an exercise in shadow and guided, low-impact contact. The purpose was to experience the interface relationship symbolically and physically. The most effective encounters in the exercise, as were revealed in the debriefing with the instructor at the conclusion, were those in which both partners to the "fight" were present and assertive, without harming the partner. The participants experienced effective sparring as a metaphor for dialogue. The least effective encounters experienced were those in which either one party over-powered the other, both parties were somewhat passive or both parties became overly aggressive. The exercise also served another purpose—it provided a physical release from the mental work that had been consuming everyone in their discussions.

This meeting would mark the beginning of a new era—one of partnership between the two organizations. They committed that together they would support the growth in the market place; their roles and competencies were complementary. Central Marketing would focus mostly on strategy and the Country Retailers would focus mostly on implementation. Both groups began to learn to become open to feedback if and when they relapsed into old behaviors.

Interface Workshop
Greenfields Central Marketing with Country Retailers
... March Year 2

Purpose

- For the Central Marketing team and the Country Retail teams to assume, collective and individual ownership and leadership for the management of their very critical interface

- In this context the workshop aims to create:
    - ✓ What added value to Greenfields is created through the interface between central and country marketing roles
    - ✓ The mutual understanding regarding the way-we-work, i.e.:
        - o How do we work in Central Marketing
        - o How do we work in Country Retailing
        - o How do Central Marketing and Country Retailing divide activities and decision making authorities (e.g. Annual Plan process, Brand Development process, Innovation process, Media Management
        - o Which are the critical steps to make this happen

Conclusions from the Team and Interface Meetings

The cycle of meetings with the individual teams and between the teams of the Senior Management Team members served to further clarify and align the new organization conceptually, emotionally and behaviorally. The enthusiasm and energy for the new organization began to emerge. And the behaviors between individuals became more constructive. The organization was mobilizing to implement the new Urgent Vision.

Maintaining momentum;
Senior Management Team Meeting II—March, Year 2

The second Senior Management Team Meeting represented a "book end" to the meeting process of the prior months. Its purpose was to take stock of merger activities to date and plan the next steps required to launch the new organization. The meeting proceeded smoothly and without event with one exception. Leonard took ill on the second day and had to leave. The Senior Management Team continued without him and completed the entire agenda, a testimony to their growth as a leadership team. The team concluded that their new organization was being properly implemented with widespread understanding, buy-in and commitment.

In a follow-up conversation between the Leonard and Arri, they concluded that this would complete Arri's involvement at this stage and they would touch base once again in the autumn to explore possible next steps in the collaboration.

Senior Management Team Meeting II
. . . March Year 2
Purpose:
To further energize the collective and individual leadership of
Multinational X Acquisition A Region Y
Review progress against decisions and actions following the December
Senior Management Team Meeting, with a focus on the organization
design and operating framework
Agree and prioritize the next phase of the merger process
Agree and decide the strategic direction of Greenfields
Review the way-of-working as Greenfields Senior Management Team

---

A new beginning;
Leonard resigns for personal reasons and is replaced by a new CEO—August Year 2

The new CEO, Julio, contracts with Arri to continue supporting the implementation of the new organization

At the end of August, Year 2, Arri received a call from the HR director that the new CEO, Julio, would like to meet him since he was evaluating how he would take the organization forward. When they met Arri reviewed the work he had done with the organization over the prior year and explained the underlying Genesis methodology. He stressed that in his view the next phase would require attention to help individual leaders and managers align their behaviors and overcome dysfunctionalities that were still hindering implementation of the new organization. Julio was genuinely curious about all that had been done in the prior year and the underlying concepts and methods.

Shortly thereafter, Julio decided to invite Arri to continue working with the organization in the next phases of implementation. He wanted to build on the progress of the past year with continuity in the approach. The HR Director reported that Julio's decision was greeted by his Senior Management Team with relief and admiration that he had the self-confidence to continue working with the process and the consultant of his predecessor.

Mobilizing the organization—the next round of interviews and Leadership Conference II—November Year 2

The next steps of the process were aimed at diagnosing the current needs of the organization in order to continue to enhance performance and implement the vision. The first step, once again, would be a round of interviews to be conducted by Arri with a sample of 30 diverse members of the organization. The next step would be to share and discuss the interview results with the top three levels of the organization, or approximately 70 individuals at the second Leadership Conference (November Year 2). This process would set the agenda for the next steps of the development of the organization.

The interview questions included:

- What are the business challenges? Are we capable to achieve them?
- What is the added value of being one, regional organization?
- Are roles, responsibilities and decision making authorities clear, nationally, regionally and across processes and functions?
- What is the overall atmosphere/mood in the organization?
- What behavior is helping / hindering delivering results?
- How is the leadership style developing?

The design for the Leadership Conference included time for small groups to explore and discuss the interview findings. In addition, once again, the martial arts exercise was introduced so that participants could physically experience the notion of constructive sparring. In the evening, the members of the Senior Management Team met apart from the other participants and made personal commitments in terms of "I will" statements regarding how they would support the further development of trusting relationships across the organization. The next day they shared their conclusions with their colleagues. The effect was to strengthen the image of the Senior Leadership Team and instil a sense of confidence the organization was being led well from top.

The interview findings were confirmed and enriched. First, it was widely agreed that the organization and the operating framework, including the processes and the roles were all relatively clear after the various steps taken over the prior year. Yet, it was also widely agreed that the behaviors were still not sufficiently supportive of delivering the planned objectives. There still was too much "silo" behavior. While the Senior Leadership Team was appearing to be more cohesive during the conference, there still was a sense that even Senior Leadership Team members were demonstrating turf protection and contributing to conflict. People referred to this as the "absence of a service mentality". An emerging consensus was that the essential next step for the organization would be to continue to build trusting relationships and be sure that colleagues could trust one another to do their part on time and according to standard all aimed at delivering the business results.

Given the success of two annual Leadership Conferences, Julio, the new CEO and the Senior Management Team decided to establish the conference as a permanent structure within the organization design, to be referred to as the "Leadership Council". Its primary purpose would be to mobilize the key leaders of the business on the business priorities as established by the Senior Management Team.

Establishing how to lead by example;
Senior Management Team Meeting III—February Year 3

With the renewed focus on aligning behaviors, Julio and the SVP of Human Resources decided to continue to develop the Senior Management Team to lead the organization by example. They agreed with Arri that the approach would entail an examination of how to improve the effectiveness of the relationships between and among the Senior Management Team members by addressing their behavior with one another. That is, they would use the meeting as the opportunity to support one another to realize the fullest of each individual's potential, as well as the potential of the team as a unit. The process would involve each team member giving and receiving feedback for learning, once again, culminating in personal commitments from each team member in the form of "I will" statements.

The meeting began with the Senior Management Team assessing its effectiveness in general terms, as a team, in terms of the criteria established by the parent company. Next the ground rules for feedback and the format to be used for the personal feedback sessions were introduced by Arri.

Ground rules for feedback and learning to lead by example

- Each team member would be the receiver of feedback while in the "hot chair".
- A fellow team member would serve as the scribe and record the feedback as it was given.
- Feedback would be descriptive of the behavior(s) of the receiver on the job which were perceived to have hindered the effectiveness of the Senior Management Team or the individual giving the feedback.
- Feedback would be non-judgmental, without attributions as to motives and without accusations.
- Questions of clarification by the receiver were encouraged during the feedback giving process.
- After all the feedback was given the team would take a break and the receiver of the feedback would reflect on the feedback and decide the key learnings which the receiver found to be valid.
- The receiver would then summarize the learning in terms of "I will" statements.
- The principle of free and informed choice guided the exercise. The feedback was not to be coercive.

During the majority of time in the meeting, the members shared the challenging and illuminating task of giving one another feedback on their respective behaviors. Their shared aim was to improve the trust in and the effectiveness of their relationships with one another in order to strengthen the performance of the business.

It was the process of sharing of feedback on relational behavior which led them to the conclusion that as a problem solving team they needed to strengthen their process of understanding the bases for decisions. They saw that improving their team problem solving ability would be facilitated by strengthening their relationships. With improved trust, their dialogue on ideas would improve and consequently so would shared understanding grounded in valid information.

Once the each team member had been a receiver, the Senior Management Team turned once again to a discussion of its effectiveness as a team. They concluded that the key area for improvement as a team was the need to be more effective in the process of dialogue and problem solving. They needed to penetrate more deeply into the analysis of data and to build different, optional scenarios for action. Their commitment was to employ a more rigorous process of achieving understanding before taking decisions grounded in their trusting relationships with one another.

Arri reported "feeling grateful at the end for having been in a position to facilitate such a deeply honest and effective process", which "represented a unique contact between human beings". He observed a strengthening of the bonds between and among the members of the team.

In mutual agreement with the Julio, Arri withdrew from active involvement with the organization once again, until such time as the Julio and his colleagues might perceive a need for the resumption of his support.

Building bridges; Interface Meeting: Greenfields Central Marketing and Country Retail Organizations II—September Year 3

The next request from the Julio to Arri concerned the need to support the implementation of the new marketing organization, once again at the interface between those serving in the corporate (central) marketing function and those serving in the various country marketing functions. (See above; Interface Meeting: Greenfields Central Marketing and Country Retail Organizations— . . . March Year 2) While the organization design, roles and decision making authorities had been agreed during the past phases of the overall transformation process, there still were concerns that the behaviors of the individuals in the various marketing organizations were not fulfilling the agreements. Results and the associated performance of the individuals were seen as sub-optimal with too much friction and misunderstanding. The first meeting between the two organizational units had not completely established the collaboration that the Julio was hoping for. The approach to the meeting was similar to the prior Senior Management Team meeting.

Objectives of the Marketing interface Meeting

- To support each other in realizing our individual and collective potential
- Individually—by receiving and giving collegial feedback (How do we as colleagues perceive each other's performance—in content and in style—and what do we recommend to one another in order to further grow and realize the potential we each have?)
- Collectively—by understanding the strengths and weaknesses of the way we operate and interact as Marketing people
- To identify actions for personal growth and the development of team performance
- Personal—bringing the "I-will-statements" from November Year 2 to a deeper level
- Team—defining behavior oriented "we-will-statements"
- With recognition of the needs of the Greenfields business
- With respect for the personal boundaries of each individual

---

Once again, the process of carefully guided giving and receiving individual feedback provided the team members to gain new insights about their own and one another's behaviors and the unintended impact they were having on one another. The results, as reported by the participants, included: stronger mutual understanding and bonding; clear "I will" commitments from individuals to change aspects of their behavior in order to foster stronger collaboration; and a shared understanding of how they could strengthen their performance as marketing colleagues even though some worked in central marketing and some worked in the marketing functions of the individual countries.

Arri reported that he felt moved by the experience of being able to contribute to the learning and the bonding within the marketing team, which for all concerned was unique. In his view, a fundamental aspect of the effectiveness of the process was the adherence to the ground rule of respect for the free and informed personal choice by each of the participants.

**Mobilizing the Organization;
Leadership Conference III—November Year 3—Entrepreneurship and Interdependency**

Julio invited Arri back again at the year end to facilitate the third annual Leadership Conference. The Senior Management Team determined the focus this time to be on energizing the individual employee for delivery of his or her own responsibilities and do this in full contact with his colleagues. The theme for this third Leadership Conference would be "entrepreneurship and interdependency".

The purposes of Leadership Conference III

- Stimulate coherence, cooperation and commitment across Multinational X/ Region Y
- Energize the personal ownership and commitment for the individual and collective results (financial and non-financial)
- Strengthen the annual plans and actions required within and across the Country Organizations and Region Y in order to realize the (financial and non-financial) targets of the business through:
- Ensuring a deep understanding of the total picture as well as the challenges of all individual functions and sectors of the business (Country Operations, and central functions, including HR, Supply Chain and Finance)
- Capitalizing on and cross-fertilizing the knowledge and experience of the participants

---

The agenda included the playing of the game Risk, as a catalyst for the exploration of personal entrepreneurship. In addition, each function and sector presented plans and received feedback from the colleagues on strengths and weaknesses. The dialogue continued to highlight key learning. The simple and focused agenda produced the intended outcomes according to the participants.

As an additional outcome people mentioned their explicit appreciation for these Leadership Conferences. Knowing that they would be involved in and consulted about the major business topics increased the level of trust in the leadership. Dialogue by now had become a part of the organization's culture.

Building leadership effectiveness;
Coaching of Senior Management Team Members Year 4-Year 5

The next phase of the transformation process built upon the personal feedback on behavior that the Senior Management Team members had shared with one another during their meeting back in February of Year 3 and the follow up activities that flowed from that meeting. Each of the Senior Management Team members worked with Arri as their personal coach every six to eight weeks with the aim being to explore more deeply their personal behavior, why they engage in behaviors which are sometimes sub-optimal and how to make appropriate, personal behavioral changes.

Continuing to strengthen the top team;
Senior Management Team Meeting IV—March Year 4

The New CEO was now using regular, yearly Senior Management Team meetings to review the performance of the business, the results and the functioning of the Senior Management Team, in terms of the quality of the relationships on the team. He decided early in Year 4 that the Senior Management Team and the organization could benefit from another Senior Management Team Meeting which would reflect on their progress in leading the organization. They would review their agreements from their last Senior Management Team meeting a year earlier. Once again he asked Arri to prepare and facilitate the meeting.

The objectives agreed were as follows:

- To support each other in better understanding our individual and collective potential
- Individually—by receiving and giving collegial feedback
- Collectively—by understanding the strengths/weaknesses of the way we operate as the Senior Management Team
- To identify actions for personal growth and growth in performance as a team
- Personal—update the "I-will-statements" from last year
- Team—review last year's "we-will-statements" and define new ones for the coming year
- Review and modify as needed the fit between our strategic (brand) focus and the design of our organization

Homework for all Senior Management Team members:

- Review everyone's "I-will-statements" of Feb Year 3
- Prepare feedback for each colleague

- To personally review progress of the Senior Management Team versus last year's "we-will-statement"

Arri reported that the Senior Management Team felt proud of its accomplishments both in terms of the trust they had developed with one another and the unity they had achieved in leading the business as one senior management team. They also identified areas for continuous improvement. They particularly challenged themselves with the necessity to energize their own direct reports to be more effective in energizing the next level of the organization, i.e., the direct reports of the Senior Management Team's direct reports.

The New CEO, the Senior Management Team and Arri also agreed that the next annual Leadership Conference (IV) would be led and facilitated by the Senior Management Team itself. Arri's only involvement would be to collaborate in the design. The organization was weaning itself from Arri's consultant/facilitation support.

Throughout the period of the transformation process, the financial results continued to improve. There was a conviction shared by the Senior Management Team that the transformation process was a key factor in the ever-improving business results. This was inter-related with the continuous learning the Senior Management Team and other levels of management had experienced in terms of the business, its organization, their individual behaviors and their team behaviors.

The Genesis Principles of Organizational Transformation and the Case: A comprehensive, multi-year process of continuous organizational improvement

The support for the development of trusting relationships characterized the almost four years of this comprehensive process of continuous organizational improvement, between the consultant, Arri, and the clients, including the CEOs (the two of them) and the management team, as well as between and among the management team members and their direct reports. The two successive CEOs led the process of transformation with sufficient bottom up input, that their behavior strengthened the development of trust throughout the organizational system. The macro process evolved over time with meetings which engaged the senior management team, the management teams who reported to the members of the senior team, leadership conferences which involved all members of the top three levels of management of the company, as well as individual coaching sessions between Arri and members of the senior management team. Multiple moments of shared awareness were manifest throughout the process.

All of the phases of dialogue unfolded as commitment was mobilized continuously-first to design and implement the merger and later to sustain the continuous improvement of the organization. Both strategic and relational meetings were employed and consistently manifested the ground rules of strategic and relational dialogue. The barriers to dialogue, with differences in perception of reality and associated action learning, were dramatically in evidence in the meetings which, in the first year integrated the two merged companies, and later brought together the central and country marketing teams. Action learning was also in evidence throughout the process, on the part of individuals who strengthened their leadership, teams which strengthened their collaboration and the organization as a whole which strengthened its coordinated performance. The action learning process was stimulated by activities which provided participants with experiences which highlighted the emotional aspects of relationships through singing and martial arts, as well as with multiple opportunities for personal feedback.

The development and implementation of the operating framework for the newly merged company employed the Genesis Urgent Vision model as the tool to address the entire organizational system and established clear boundaries for dialogue on different levels of the hierarchy. The senior management team developed the overall organizational operating framework and the individual department management teams proceeded to develop the details within that framework. The goals of the organizational transformation were realized as the results of the business continued to improve thus realizing the leveraging of total resources of the system while strengthening individual capabilities through the ongoing learning process. The resilience of the organizational system, including all sub-systems and their interrelationships was continuously strengthened over the course of the transformation process.

Chapter 12
Globalization
Facilitating a macro process which mobilizes commitment

Introduction

MNX in Year One had begun to address the potential for significant cost-saving and efficiencies in its multi-billion Euro Corp purchasing operations, around the world. This was another step in its continuing process to adapt its global organization to the competitive demands of the global economy. Continuing through Year Six, Genesis consultant, Michael Manolson, consulted with MNX's purchasing operations to help them transform their organization, processes and culture to deliver the expected global efficiencies. Through Year Five, Michael supported the globalization of the purchasing organization in one of MNX's two Divisions, Division I, under the leadership of the Vice President, Global Purchasing, whom we shall call Ludwig. In Year Five, MNX's senior management decided to integrate Purchasing Division I with Purchasing in MNX's second Division, Division II. Michael supported that integration process as well, continuing into Year Six, with Ludwig assuming leadership of the combined operations.

Ludwig called upon Michael for assistance since they had already worked together in the client-consultant relationship successfully and developed trust in one another. Ludwig knew that he was being greeted by his colleagues with suspicion and resistance. He came from a background outside of purchasing. His new colleagues felt he could not understand their work. They were also explicitly averse to the overall goal to globalize their operations. Each one was a lead buyer in one of the major regions of the world and enjoyed considerable power, autonomy and the perks that came with the authority to make decisions involving huge sums of money. They would now be expected to relinquish some control over their regional operations and share buying with colleagues in other regions. While senior management decision to globalize was clear and the significant financial benefits to MNX were obvious to all—savings that would exceed a billion Euros due to volume discounts and increased buying leverage with suppliers—the emotional resistance of the regional buyers was high.

The barriers to establishing the global supplier organization also came from outside the circle of regional buyers. Each had a solid line reporting relationship to a boss in the home region. As was later revealed, while all of the bosses in their regional organizations publicly supported the establishment of Global Purchasing, some privately they opposed the idea. In at least one instance a regional purchasing manager had been instructed to ignore global targets and focus only on delivering regional targets.

The regional purchasing managers also resented what they perceived as contradictory messages from senior management: "globalize, but . . ." MNX had already taken significant steps to globalize marketing, R&D, HR and other functions. Purchasing resided within the manufacturing organization and MNX was slow to globalize manufacturing. Manufacturing was not given a seat with the Senior Leadership Team which ran MNX. The Regional Presidents, who were members of the MNX Senior Leadership Team, were the reason. They wanted to control manufacturing within each of their respective regions, ostensibly in order to control all elements of the P/L statements for which they were being held accountable. Consequently, the regional purchasing managers were told on the one hand, "globalize" and on the other hand, "your parent organization, manufacturing, will remain regionalized."

Heightening the difficulty of his new job, Ludwig was not given line authority over the group. Instead, he was expected to be the primus inter pares (first among equals). Without more formal authority, he knew from the beginning that he could not simply impose his will; instead he would have to engage his colleagues collaboratively and use constructive influence to win them over.

Chronology of the Macro Process	
Defining the framework for the new, global Purchasing organization; Division I Global Purchasing Leadership Team Meeting I	May, Year One

Defining the framework for the new, global Purchasing organization with next level managers; Division I Global Purchasing Leadership Team Meeting II	June, Year One
Sharpening the way of working; Division I Global Purchasing Leadership Team Meeting III	September, Year One
Building Bridges; The Division I Global Purchasing Leadership Team and The R&D Organization Interface Meetings	December, Year One; May, Year Two; December Year Two
How are we doing? Division I Purchasing Evaluation of the Pilot Global Purchasing teams	October, Year Two
Launching the expansion of the number of global purchasing teams; The Division I Global Purchasing Launch Meeting	April, Year Four
The plot thickens; Division I and Division II Purchasing Organizations begin to integrate	December, Year Four
Doing the work of integration; MNX decides to integrate the two Purchasing organizations of Division I and Division II	
Four meetings with the new MNX Purchasing Leadership Team	September, Year Five; October, Year Five; November, Year Five; February, Year Six
One "rollout" meeting with the direct reports of the MNX Purchasing Leadership Team—approximately 100 middle managers	March, Year Six

Defining the framework for the new, global Purchasing organization; Division I Global Purchasing Leadership Team Meeting I—May Year One

Ludwig commenced his new assignment by establishing a Global Purchasing Leadership Team, comprising all of the regional purchasing managers. He next contracted with Michael to build the team and the plan by which they would integrate their regional purchasing operations into one global purchasing organization. Employing the Genesis approach, Michael conducted a round of interviews of all of the members of the Global Purchasing Leadership Team, wrote a synthesis of the interviews and developed a detailed agenda for a two day meeting. The aim of the meeting would be to review debate and agree elements of the framework for the Global Purchasing Leadership Team's organization and work going forward. The proposed decision making process was consensus. Ludwig had no ultimate decision making authority. The process permitted Ludwig to advocate for his views while the facilitator, Michael, would assure that all views were heard and consensus was followed as the decision making mode. The proposed framework for designing the new organization would follow the Genesis Urgent Vision model (Chapter 9).

The specific objectives of Global Purchasing Leadership Team Meeting I

- Continue the process of building the new global Division I Global Purchasing Leadership Team based on trust and a thorough understanding of the needs of the individual members, their regional purchasing organizations, Division I as a total entity and MNX as a whole
- Collaboratively develop the Urgent Vision framework (draft I) of the Division I Global Purchasing Leadership Team
- Reaffirm the Terms of Reference (initial job descriptions) and Guiding Principles
- Re-clarify the brief for the Pilot Global Purchasing Teams (established in certain areas of material buying to demonstrate the potential of Global Purchasing)
- Identify the priority problems in key business processes for Global Purchasing
- Review the objectives for the next meeting to be held in September. This would entail the development of the Operating Framework, a full description of how the new Global Purchasing Leadership Team would operate based on the Urgent Vision.

The May Year One meeting represented the launch of the new Global Purchasing Leadership Team and was also the first meeting with Ludwig in the job as head. It. Michael reported that while the Team discussed, debated and agreed all the salient points on the agenda, the process of the meeting revealed the emotional resistance of several of the members, including an array of dysfunctional meeting behaviors. There were side conversations, silences, changing of the topic, challenges to the agenda and direct criticisms of Michael, alleging he was pushing Ludwig's agenda.

Nonetheless, Ludwig and Michael persevered. The meeting process included all elements of the Urgent Vision framework for review, as described in the interview synthesis. Step by step the team was facilitated to highlight initial points of agreement and debate points of disagreement until agreement was found. In spite of the resistant behavior of some of the Global Purchasing Leadership Team members, Ludwig and Michael worked closely together to listen to the objections, challenge them where appropriate and maintain the momentum of the meeting.

At the end of the meeting, the team members reported that the interviews, as captured in the interview synthesis, helped accelerate and deepen the meeting dialogue. Each member felt listened to. By being interviewed individually and anonymously they had been able to reveal openly more of their thoughts and feelings than they would have felt comfortable doing in the meeting. The constraints to openness in the first meeting were considerable, given the resistance described above and newness of the team. Most of the team members did not know each other well. The team members also reported that the process of the meeting was effective. By reviewing, debating and ultimately agreeing, by consensus, on key elements of the Urgent Vision, they felt understanding, buy-in and commitment to their shared work.

The effective meeting process had been necessary, yet not sufficient to account for the progress which they had achieved. The members of the Global Purchasing Leadership Team knew that the senior management of MNX expected the globalization process to go forward and succeed. The Team members knew, even with their reservations, that they did not have the option of not cooperating.

The Urgent Vision which the team agreed in this first meeting proved durable over the succeeding years. As intended, it became the basis for the Operating Framework and was repeatedly referenced by purchasing managers all over the world on various levels of authority.

Defining the framework for the new, global Purchasing organization with next level managers;
Division I Global Purchasing Leadership Team Meeting II—June 14, 15, Year One

Ludwig and the Global Purchasing Leadership Team agreed to continue the process of developing themselves as a team and designing their new global purchasing organization with another meeting.

The objectives for the next meeting

- Continue the process of building the new Division I Global Purchasing Leadership Team based on trust and a thorough understanding of the needs of the individual members, their organizations and Division I as a total entity
- Validate the Global Purchasing Leadership Team's Urgent Vision, job descriptions (Terms of Reference) and Strategy
- Identify and resolve priority issues facing Teams in the next 3-4 months
- Clarify decision making authorities in the key business process steps relevant to the pilot Global Purchasing Teams' work in the next 3-4 months
- Agree the process going forward

The output of the May Global Purchasing Leadership Team meeting was reviewed and refined effectively. The members reported appreciation of having another iteration of discussions on this complex set of important issues. The process deepened their shared understanding, buy-in and commitment.

The Global Purchasing Leadership Team also invited next level managers, the Pilot Team leaders, to join them for a second part of the meeting. The Pilot Team leaders had been assigned to lead the first round of cross-regional, global purchasing projects through Global Executive Buying Teams. Their presence produced several benefits both "soft" and "hard". First, the Pilot Team members came to learn more concretely what was expected of them and the entire global purchasing community, by reviewing the work done by the Leadership Team. Next, the Pilot Team members felt included recognized and respected, which enhanced their motivation to do their part of the transformation. Finally, the meeting provided an opportunity for relationships to develop among managers who shared global objectives, yet rarely saw each other or even had direct contact with one another in the day to day routine of their work.

Sharpening the way of working;
Division I Global Purchasing Leadership Team Meeting III—September, Year One

The next step of the process of building the new Global Purchasing Leadership Team and its complete Global Purchasing organization would be to build on the Urgent Vision work of the prior meetings and develop the details of the Operating Framework. The focus would be on designing a globally consistent buying process and the associated roles and decision authorities. Instead of each region using its own approach, together the team would design one global approach. In addition, the Urgent Vision framework would be reviewed one more time and modified as needed. The output of the meeting also included agreements on various actions pertaining to the actual work of Global Purchasing with regard to issues concerning their suppliers.

A turning point in the gelling of the Global Purchasing Leadership Team came in this meeting. One of the members, whom we shall call Luigi, reported that his regional boss privately had been instructing him to focus only on regional priorities and ignore the global priorities of the Global Purchasing Leadership Team. Luigi asked his global purchasing colleagues for help on how to manage his regional boss, pursue the global priorities and keep his job. Over time, he succeeded on all counts.

During this period the membership of the Global Purchasing Leadership Team also went through a change. One of the regional buyers who had had the most difficulty adjusting to the global role and had continued his subtle resistance throughout the prior meetings finally retired. Working with him had required significant effort. On several occasions in the course of the meetings he had tried to renege on prior commitments. Repeatedly, he conceded when the notes clearly showed what he had previously actually said and agreed to. Ludwig expressed gratitude for the Genesis methodology which yielded the simple and powerful tool of accurate meeting notes. The facilitator captured the dialogue of important meeting conversations real time through transcription on a lap top connected to a projector so that all participants could see what was written; in essence, using the computer like a flip chart, only more rigorously.

To assure effective implementation of the various organizational and business decisions, Ludwig instituted a bi-weekly Global Purchasing Leadership Team conference call to follow-up on the details and assure that each individual was delivering on personal commitments. Given that each of the Global Purchasing Leadership Team members also had their own regional responsibilities, they agreed that the disciplined, bi-weekly follow up was important to effective implementation and the maintenance of momentum.

Building Bridges;
The Division I Global Purchasing Leadership Team and the R&D Organization Interface Meetings—December Year One; May Year Two; December Year Two

Ludwig and the Global Purchasing Leadership Team were eager to address the important interdependence between their process of purchasing of raw materials and the innovation process of research and development. The right materials, at the right cost, at the right time would be essential to the success of new product development.

They were keenly aware that their organization of buyers around the world was perceived by the rest of the organization, including those working on innovation, as operating in isolation, a "tribe unto itself". Their focus traditionally had been principally external; they had consistently tended to spend more time with suppliers whom they were continually looking to "squeeze" than with colleagues in the business who depended on the deals they made. This culture had built up considerable frustration especially with the R&D colleagues. R&D depended partnership relationships with strategic suppliers in order that the experimentation of finding the right materials for the desired specifications would happen effectively, efficiently, fast and at good cost levels. Due to the modus operandi of Purchasing, R&D had not been able to optimize these partnerships. Finally, the Global Purchasing Leadership Team was ready to collaborate fully with R&D.

The Global Purchasing Leadership Team took the initiative to host the first meeting with R&D in December, Year One. The participants would comprise the lead managers from both organizations.

- Category Research and Development Directors, with prime responsibility for defining the strategic needs of the new product to be developed from a category perspective (Note: a category represented a cluster of brands and products defined by a market niche)
- Global Technology Center Heads, with responsibility to perform the actual development work in the laboratories
- Category Vice Presidents of Manufacturing with responsibility for oversight and management of all manufacturing matters pertaining to a category, including incoming raw materials, the manufacture and packaging of the product, inventory and final distribution to the customers.

The December Year One Purchasing—R&D Meeting would be the first of three such meetings. The Global Purchasing Leadership Team would continue the process by hosting the next meetings in May, Year Two and December Year Two. The team continued to role model the benefits of developing global organizations and global processes as a means of leveraging the resources of the global enterprise in order to strengthen performance.

The first meeting employed some Genesis tools to support the development of new collaborations. One exercise focused on "Expects from/ Provides to", a simple process where each sub-group developed its description of what it expected from its new counterparts and what it would provide to them. The exercise resulted in considerable, substantive action planning on many of the important business issues which the different participants shared with one another.

The second meeting was held only six months after the first and included sixty participants, 15 from the R&D community and 45 from the Purchasing global community, including the Global Purchasing Leadership Team.

The agreed summary of the meeting, as created by the participants themselves in the form of an "elevator speech" stated:

"The May Year Two meeting of representatives from the Category R&D and Manufacturing functions and Global Purchasing was a success in designing and strengthening the Interface between Division I R&D and Purchasing. Following up on the December meeting, working groups made recommendations on the way forward and these were refined and endorsed by the Category Research and Development Directors, the Global Technology Center Heads, and the VP Manufacturing. Since much of the meeting was devoted to working groups developing plans on specific topics, the output was rich in substance and covered a wide range of topics, covering both the details of working on material strategies and buying, as well as on the organizational issues of the coordination of roles, communications and decision making between the R&D community and the Purchasing community. The participants felt that their productivity had been high and their ability to continue to develop trust across the organizational and geographic boundaries continued grow."

One key meeting activity involved all meeting participants from both organizations in updating and endorsing the materials strategy process and the associated decision authorities in the decision grid, i.e., who would decide what and who would consult with whom and who would be informed of decisions.

The relationships between the R&D and the Purchasing participants were also strengthened by a specific exercise whereby the participants described the behaviors (e.g., team working, seeking help when needed, etc.) and organizational elements (e.g. objectives, priority setting, project work) they observed were working well and those that needed to change.

A more detailed summary of the meeting was also developed

What we did:
Renewed and deepened the friendship between ourselves and our two communities
Built relationships that will enable us to deliver further than the roles we put down on paper.
Committed to some specific actions that we will implement going further.
What we commit to do:
Focus on our own behavior
Behave the way we want others to behave
Maturity
Better decision making
Get through the MNX disease (i.e., decisions taken with poor implementation)
Work to decision
Make the right decision and then figure out ways to sort out any individual problems that might arise
Create the pull rather than the push
Let's look for challenging opportunities in the material strategies and executive teams that we will pilot
Push the boundaries
Change the process
Celebrate and lead through success

The third meeting was held one year after the first one—in December, Year Two. The participants were, with few exceptions, the same as the first meeting. After one year of working together the consensus was that, while they had made progress, their joint process of developing material strategies still needed to be improved. The meeting devoted considerable, productive attention to developing a new and strengthened approach to the joint material strategy and decision making process. It was widely felt that the work would contribute both to improving the innovation process, as well as to strengthening the effectiveness of Purchasing.

How are we doing?
Division I Purchasing Evaluation of the Pilot Global Purchasing teams—October, Year Two

Ludwig and the Global Purchasing Leadership Team next conducted an evaluation of the progress of the 6 Pilot Global Purchasing teams via interviews and a questionnaire which Michael's support. The respondents were individuals from various functions from all geographies around the world who interfaced with the buying function in some way.

Overall, the progress of the pilot teams and the management and leadership by the Global Purchasing Leadership Team was found to be overwhelmingly positive as the following representative quotes indicate:

"I have observed an impressive acceleration of change in last months, in steps that been fudged in other areas of the organization. For example; the closeness of the way Global Purchasing Leadership Team has been working (they have met 7 or 8 times this year, and are on the phone every two weeks), and the quality of information in the last 6 months has also increased hugely reflecting an information flow coming up from the pilot teams to the Global Purchasing Leadership Team and out into the business."
"It has gone well, been led well. It is one of the better stories in MNX about where we have gone global."

"One of the best MNX processes managed on a global basis, in contrast to some where we are trying and they are not working so well—such as innovation. We have experienced significant savings that we could not have achieved without this process."

"I am very pleased with the progress we have made in several supply areas, and I hope that we can match that with similar initiatives in more supply areas next year."

"I feel that Ludwig and the Global Purchasing Leadership Team have done a tremendous amount in a short period of time."

Based on the evaluation, the Global Purchasing Leadership Team proposed to their superiors, the members of the Manufacturing Leadership Team, to expand the 6 pilot Global Purchasing teams to 21. The proposal was approved.

**Launching the expansion of the number of global purchasing teams;
The Division I Global Purchasing Launch Meeting—April, Year Four**

Now that the Global Purchasing Teams had expanded in number,
Ludwig and the Global Purchasing Leadership Team agreed that all
of the global teams should come together to continue to refine their
process of working; identify and plan improvements; and strengthen
the collegiality of the global supplier community. The preparation of
the meeting included a round of interviews by Michael with the Global
Purchasing Leadership Team and other team leaders, as well as series
of discussions between and among Ludwig, Michael and the Global
Purchasing Leadership Team to design the agenda.

The week of meetings began on the first evening, with a joint meeting of
the Global Purchasing Leadership Team and the next level of managers,
the leaders of the Global Purchasing teams and continued for the full
next day. The purpose was to strengthen the working relationship of the
two top layers of management of the entire Global Purchasing operation
and to prepare for their roles in leading the full community of global
teams for the follow-on meeting over the next two days. The understood
how important their leadership would be to the overall success of the
portfolio of teams around the world.

During the first meeting, the Global Purchasing Leadership Team and the
Purchasing Team Leaders were able to identify blocks and obstacles and
means to resolve them. They also spent time getting to know each other
better as individuals so they could be more effective as the expanded
leadership team of Global Purchasing. They also prepared themselves
for the roles they would play in the follow-on meeting with the full
membership of the Global Purchasing teams.

The preparation proved to be invaluable. During the full meeting over the
next two days there were various moments that the Global Purchasing
Leadership Team was on the podium together interacting and responding
to questions with the full audience of approximately 100 supply managers
from around the world. It was reported by several attendees how obvious
it was to all that the Global Purchasing Leadership Team was aligned
and working effectively with one another. Questions were answered
effectively and colleagues on the Global Purchasing Leadership Team

would support one another in amplifying answers. The first day of the full meeting had all members working in plenary and in teams on selected topics of interest to all. To further reinforce the importance of the initiative within the broader strategy of the corporation, the senior executive above the Global Purchasing Leadership Team, the head of the Global Manufacturing organization of which Purchasing was a part, helped introduce the meeting. He provided a broad strategic overview of Manufacturing and the role that Purchasing played within it. The final day was devoted to each Global Purchasing team working together on its own issues to take advantage of being face to face.

The plot thickens;
Division I and Division II Purchasing Organizations begin to integrate—December, Year Four

MNX began to embark on a further integration of the operations of the two Divisions, Division I and Division II, by the end of Year Four. The two Global Purchasing Leadership Teams were requested by their Manufacturing superiors to engage in an exploratory meeting on how best to integrate their two operations. The co-sponsors of the meeting were the superiors of the two Global Purchasing Leadership Teams, the two SVPs of Manufacturing for Division I and Division II. The SVP of Manufacturing in Division I had an additional role; he had been appointed to be the manager of "One MNX" for Manufacturing, with the goal of integrating and harmonizing manufacturing of both Division II and Division I.

The objectives agreed for the December Integration Meeting

- Establish a common basis of understanding of how we each operate in our respective Divisions
- Identify some concrete opportunities to unlock value through joint management of materials used by both Divisions and agree an implementation plan to realize them
- Identify common gaps in Purchasing capabilities and develop a shared agenda to address them
- Agree (or agree to disagree) on some fundamental organizing principles for One MNX Purchasing across the two Divisions

No decision had yet been made on the potential structural integration of the two Purchasing organizations of Division II and Division I, although it was acknowledged by all those involved that one outcome could be a single, integrated Global Purchasing Leadership Team. There was a further, anxiety-provoking recognition that if the integration were to occur that not every member of the two Global Purchasing Leadership Teams would have a job in the future since the roles in Division II and DIVISION I were duplicative in each geography. Everyone understood that integration would lead to having only one Global Purchasing Leadership Team in each regional geography instead of the existing two.

The expectations going into the meeting were highly charged. On the one hand, all understood and accepted the potential of even greater cost savings and efficiencies and bottom line benefits for MNX. On the other hand, most everyone feared the possibility of losing his or her job. The anxiety was compounded by a history of negative perceptions between the Global Purchasing Leadership Teams of Division II and Division II as a result of their lack of contact and the prejudices which had arisen over the years between the two Divisions. The doubts regarding the feasibility of the integration were further stoked by a widespread belief that the business models of the two divisions were incompatible; Division I was believed to be well suited to global purchasing whereas Division II was believed to required local and regional purchasing since their products and brands translated less well globally and required local and regional modifications to suit consumer needs.

Once again, the preparation for the meeting began with a round of interviews by Michael. The trust reported was low between the two groups and the negative mutual attributions high. The Division II Global Purchasing Leadership Team members also reported negative perceptions of Ludwig and interpreted his proactive style as over-controlling and worse. Given the close and trusting relationship between Michael and Ludwig, Michael was able to advise Ludwig to play a low-key role in the upcoming meeting—"don't be directive; don't lecture; let me facilitate the process". Ludwig later heeded the advice. The interview synthesis held up the mirror: it presented the lack of mutual understanding and negative history forthrightly so the participants could address them as barriers to overcome.

The interviews also served as the data from which Michael facilitated the negotiations to agree on the objectives for the meeting between and among Ludwig, and the SVPs Manufacturing of the two Divisions. The output of the meeting would be reviewed by the respective Division II and Division I Senior Leadership Teams. The differences in their views added another level of complexity to the negotiations. Yet, agreement was found between the two SVPs from the two Divisions with regard to the objectives of the meeting. Overall, there was no doubt that the two divisions would merge their two purchasing organizations.

The first phase of the meeting was designed in consideration of the resistant perceptions from both sides. The Division I team's prevailing attitude towards Division II was arrogance—they saw themselves as having had much more experience with global purchasing. The Division II team's attitude towards Division I was fear—they were concerned that they would be "taken over" by Division I. They recognized that the Division I Global Purchasing Leadership Team had already spent some years building themselves as an effective team while they, the Division II Global Purchasing Leadership Team, were still a group of individuals working solely in their own regions.

The first activity of the meeting was designed so that members of the two Divisions could understand each other's perceptions. First, pairs, one Division I and one Division II Global Purchasing Leadership Team member were invited to have lunch together. The aim was to begin to get to know one another informally. Upon return from the lunch each individual reported on what they learned. This discussion progressed into a discussion of a shared vision of what the attributes of a unified Purchasing for MNX could be in five years—not yet a shared structure.

Next, the two Global Purchasing Leadership Team s were invited to meet separately and engage in a humorous exercise that would prove to be profoundly beneficial. Each group was asked to illustrate three groups with an animal as a metaphor:
Yourselves—i.e., your own Global Purchasing Leadership Team
Your counterparts—i.e., the other Global Purchasing Leadership Team
What the joint, integrated Global Purchasing Leadership Team might be

Another exercise was employed to help the members of the two Global Purchasing Leadership Teams overcome their differences. They engaged in martial arts facilitated by karate black belt who was also a psychologist. The title for the exercise was "buyers as warriors". Through the shadow boxing exercise, the karate psychologist was able to facilitate the debriefing so that the participants could understand the emotions of inter-group competition that they brought to the meeting.

The agenda design also included considerable substantive work to explore areas of collaboration and to develop action plans. At the end of the meeting, the two SVPs of Manufacturing joined and received reports from the two teams of the progress made. The reports included the animal metaphors which once again were received with laughter as well as an impressive listing of the substantive areas of prospective collaboration. The meeting was considered a remarkable success, by most everyone, both substantively as well as emotionally as relationships across the divide of the two teams had begun to develop.

Doing the work of integration;
MNX decides to integrate the two Purchasing organizations of Division I and Division II

- *Four meetings with the new MNX Purchasing Leadership Team: September, Year Five; October, Year Five; November, Year Five; February, Year Six*
- *One "rollout" meeting with the direct reports of the MNX Global Purchasing Leadership Team—approximately 100 middle managers—March Year Six*

MNX Senior Management formally decided to integrate the Division I and Division II Purchasing organizations and appointed Ludwig as the head of the new, integrated MNX Purchasing Leadership Team. Surprising to all and upsetting to Ludwig, he was not promoted to a higher salary level and still only retained the designation of primus inter pares.

Michael was invited to facilitate a series of four organizing meetings of the new MNX Global Purchasing Leadership Team with responsibility for both divisions. Once again, the focus was to help build the new management team and design how the two organizations would work together. Throughout the meetings the new Team worked step by step on their relationships, as well as on designing the details of their new organization and operating framework. They also worked to prepare for their meeting with all of their direct reports. The preparation of the leadership team for a meeting with the direct reports had proven to be a powerful technique for developing shared understanding and mobilizing the organization for implementation.

The process once again proved to energize all the participants. The remarkable five year journey of MNX's Purchasing organization to integrate and deliver cost efficiencies had been acknowledged as a resounding success across MNX. The numbers didn't lie—the savings were in the hundreds of millions of Euros. And the feelings of the participants didn't lie—they reported a highly enriching experience, while overcoming all of the complexities and the barriers of mistrust.

The Genesis Principles of Organizational Transformation and the Case: Globalizing a division of a multinational corporation

The project began with a foundation of trust that already existed between the consultant, Michael and the client, Ludwig, VP, Global Purchasing based on their significant prior work together. Time and time again, over the course of the six years of the engagement, Michael and Ludwig were able to support the global purchasing teams to overcome their suspicions and resistance. During the first five years, the Division I global purchasing team was formed and developed into a highly effective unit which led the global implementation of global purchasing and delivered the results of enormous cost savings. In the last year, they led the successful merger of the Division I and Division II global purchasing teams.

The macro process evolved over the years through a series of meetings (meetings) as Ludwig and the Division I team developed themselves first and then engaged next level teams to actually do the work of global purchasing. They also exploited the opportunity to smooth the interfaces between global purchasing and R&D, a critical relationship, since R&D made decisions regarding material selection which had significant implications for the purchasing costs. Critical moments of shared awareness emerged which demonstrated how effectively the barriers of different perceptions/different realities were overcome, as the team members overcame their regional perspective to embrace the global perspective.

Progressively, all of the phases of dialogue, principally strategic dialogue, were manifest as the senior global purchasing team mobilized commitment, including with next level teams, to deliver global purchasing and reap the rewards of significant cost savings. Action learning was also in evidence throughout the process on the part of all participants, perhaps most notably on the part of Ludwig, the leader. While he did not have line authority, with Michael's assistance, he learned to influence his colleagues to collaborate through the tools of dialogue.

The entire system of global purchasing was addressed, with the assistance of the Genesis Urgent Vision tool, including the culture of collaboration, the processes, the strategy/business model and the structure. The systems perspective included collaborating up and down the hierarchy as well as laterally across organizational boundaries with R&D. The relationship between the leadership team and the next level operational teams effectively applied the clarity of different roles by employing the principle of freedom within a framework.

The goal of the transformation, to deliver significant cost reductions through global purchasing, successfully illustrated the power of the principle, leveraging the total resources while strengthening individual capabilities. As described above (Chapter 9), the global purchasing team demonstrated significant resilience in overcoming multiple organizational challenges, including the confusing and sometimes conflicting signals from senior management in the regions and in the headquarters.

Chapter 13
Accelerated Strategy Development
Facilitating meetings employing strategic and relational dialogue

Introduction
One meeting can be pivotal for an organizational transformation, as this case illustrates. It was intended that way by the leaders who convened it. They had an urgent, significant business opportunity that they felt required immediate, intense attention, if they were to capitalize on it. Accordingly, they employed a process they knew to be effective; a project leader and facilitator in whom they had confidence and a rigorous, albeit fast, preparation phase to assure the meeting was comprehensively designed.

The two top leaders of HHM, the CEO of the holding company, HMM Global, Inc. and MJ, CEO of the subsidiary, HMM, Inc., which manufactured and marketed heavy machinery equipment, identified China as the corporation's number 1 global, strategic market growth opportunity. They decided to mobilize the organization for dramatic growth in China with the development of a China Growth strategy. They determined that as soon as possible it would be necessary to free HMM China from its position as a business unit within the administrative scope of their Eurasia Region into an independent, self standing regional business. They agreed that MJ would provide senior guidance to the process and take on the role of "sponsor". His job would be to assemble the team and assure that the methodology of strategy development selected would lead to a high probability of successful and rapid implementation. MJ began by assigning one of their high potential business directors, MS, to lead their China business and the development of its new strategy. While relatively young at 42, MS had spent many years in various HMM businesses around the world, including China.

A key reason that MJ gave MS the responsibility of leading the strategy process was that he thought that the mindset of the Eurasia Regional managers, headquartered in the UK, would not be supportive of the independence of the China Region. Without China's achieving independence as a business region he doubted that China could rapidly fulfill its growth potential. The Eurasia Regional managers had been presiding over the shrinkage of their prime business in the UK for decades. They had strived to compensate and succeeded partially by developing new businesses in Eastern Europe and Asia, including China. They considered China as their star since it already represented a significant portion of the total business for the region. Understandably, for some, there was reluctance to invest their own time and energy to make China an independent region.

MJ also recognized that the Eurasia Regional Management Team had been unable to accelerate the growth of the China business. The entrepreneurial risk taking and courage required to ensure that China would be ahead of the growth curve was foreign to the culture of caution they had learned to adopt during the past decades due to the chronic ongoing downsizing they had been forced to employ in the UK. Their learned instincts were conservatism and retrenchment rather than innovation and expansion.

The China growth strategy was so important to the business that MJ also decided which methodology to employ and he was confident that he knew what he wanted. He also was confident in his own knowledge of the Chinese and global markets and in his organization's technical capability. He wanted to assure that the strategy would be high quality and would be implemented well and quickly. For these reasons, he wanted his own managers to develop the strategic plan, to assure their own understanding, buy-in and commitment, rather than outsource the process to a consultancy, however expert and elegant the work of consultants might be.

MJ had had ample success with an intensive, cross-functional meeting method design to solve complex problems rapidly, what HMM called the 30-60-90 Process. (Note: we shall use the terms "meeting" and "meeting" interchangeably.) Based on GE's famous Workout! Methodology, the 30-60-90 Process focused on implementation of plans created in an intensive three-day meeting within 90 days, preceded by rigorous progress reviews at the 30 day and 60 day milestones. MJ had experienced the power of the methodology while leading another company before he joined HHM. He had imported the 30-60-90 Process upon his arrival some years before to overcome the HMM culture he had found to have been too cautious and slow to act. This was the process he wanted employed in the development of the China strategic plan. Given his prior experience with Kees who had successfully facilitated numerous such meetings for MJ in the past, once again he invited Kees to facilitate the process. Recognizing the importance of involving all key stakeholders across geographies and functions, MJ invited his peer, RDG, CEO of another subsidiary of the parent company, HMM Global, Inc. which manufactured and marketed related heavy machinery, also in the South-East region, to join him as co-sponsor. HMM and the partner subsidiary needed to collaborate.

MJ also decided to challenge his team with a goal that he believed was feasible, albeit extremely ambitious: 500 million Dollars in sales in China in five years, over three times the current sales volume and achievement of parity with the HMM USA business, historically, the largest regional business within HHM. He also wanted the new China region to become the primary source for components and sub-assemblies for HHM's world-wide operations. And he wanted the strategy meeting to occur in January of the coming year, only a few months away. These goals were huge and unheard of for HHM. In aggregate, they represented a long term commitment to China far beyond the next five years. He clearly communicated an Urgent Vision.

MJ had staked much in a single 3 day meeting. He put himself on the line publicly with his superior and his subordinates that the goals of growth in China would be achieved. In so doing, he also put constructive pressure on the project leader, MS, the facilitator, Kees and all the cross-functional participants who were to be invited as well as his full management team.

Investing in designing the meeting
The Preparatory Meeting—December Year 1

Given the import of the proposed China Growth strategy meeting, Kees proposed and the clients readily agreed to have a design meeting to prepare the meeting with the senior management teams of both sister companies: HMM and Q&I, including the two CEOs, MJ and RDG. The CEOs readily agreed. The China strategy was such a high priority that assuring the understanding, buy-in and commitment of their two respective management teams was essential to the success of the implementation of the strategy. They quickly settled on Johannesburg, RSA as the venue optimally accessible for all and early December as the timing, one month away. Kees would facilitate the meeting. Kees and MS would prepare the agenda. Their aim was to design the upcoming strategy meeting for optimal value and productivity. The agenda for the preparatory meeting comprised the following topics:

- Goals for the strategy
- Objective of the meeting
- Scope of the meeting
- Methodology, ground rules, agenda and Draft input document for the meeting
  (Note: the Draft input document is intended to summarize the views of the participants coming into the meeting: points of agreement and disagreement. In the meeting it serves as a catalyst for dialogue. Points may be modified, agreed or rejected with the aim being consensus.)
- Participants and roles
- Venue
- Dates
- Communications to participants in preparation for the meeting

Goals for the strategy
MJ opened the preparatory meeting by reiterating the challenging goals of the China Growth strategy:

- Grow the China business to 500 million Dollars of sales within China in five years, more than 3 times the current sales volume
- Become an independent business region within the HMM structure by FY 07, that is "spin-off" from being under the aegis of the HMM Eurasia Region
- Become the primary source for components, sub-assemblies and certain OE machines for HHM's worldwide operations. This goal illustrated HHM's long term commitment to doing business in China. This commitment would be seen by the Chinese market as a powerful gesture of good citizenship and would support HHM's bid to obtain a license to continue to operate in China
- Protect HHM's proprietary knowledge

Objective of the Meeting
MJ also reiterated that the objective of the meeting would be to develop a preliminary strategic plan and action plan to finalize the strategic plan within 90 days. The strategic plan needed to be financially robust in order to justify the anticipated significant capital and personnel investments to be made.

Scope of the Meeting
Interactively the assembled participants developed which questions would be in scope, as well as out of scope during the meeting, to assure clarity and focus on such a complex topic.

Methodology, ground rules, agenda and Draft input documents for the meeting prior to the preparatory meeting, Kees and MS deliberated on what methodology to employ within the 3 days they would have with the team. It would be a challenge to develop the preliminary strategic plan, as well as the action plan for completion of the plan over the subsequent 90 days. Conventional corporate strategy processes (e.g. by such known authors as Arnaldo Hax or Michael Porter) were data intensive, analytic, time consuming (typically consuming months), expensive and labor intensive, frequently employing external consultants. These strategy processes would not work. The time was too limited across all phases—the preparation, the 3 day meeting and the 90 day period. And there was MJ's further requirement to develop the strategic plan with managers who later would lead the implementation and not rely on outside consultants.

They settled on a simple methodology that would form the basis for the 3 day agenda and which Kees had employed over the years in multiple meetings, with similar constraints and conditions, with consistent success:
What are our objectives?
What is the current reality?
What is our desired state?
What actions do we need to achieve the desired state?

They also recognized that there were risks with this methodology. The participants would be asked to work in ways which were foreign to them. In the more conventional strategy processes it is common that the marketing strategy is developed first and then is used as input to the other strategies sequentially, including manufacturing, sourcing, HR, finance, IT, R&D, etc. over months. As needed, the cycle is repeated iteratively to achieve alignment among all the components. Given the constraints of 3 days for the meeting, the different functional disciplines would have to work in parallel rather than in sequence to develop their component strategic plans. They hoped and trusted that the participants would be willing to work in this unconventional manner and that the resultant different functional plans would fit together sufficiently that the participants would feel motivated by their agreements to proceed. There was a risk that the different plans could evolve as dramatically opposed or out of alignment with one another and the exercise would fail.

To support the limited time for developing the preliminary strategic plans, Kees proposed to MS the development of input documents in a few priority topic areas which in Genesis we refer to as Strawman documents, while brief, would serve to help orient the participants to the conversation and help accelerate the dialogue by providing baseline data and codification of existing ideas held by management. They were to be considered catalysts for the dialogue, not formal proposals. With a preparatory team, Kees facilitated the making of a Draft sourcing make-buy strategy input document based on MS's knowledge plus the input of a few sourcing and manufacturing managers. MS prepared a Draft 5-year sales outlook based on his own knowledge and the input of a few marketing managers. Kees knew that by preparing the Draft not only was he providing a useful tool for the meeting, he also was educating himself on an important content question which would enable him to be even more effective as a facilitator—he would really understand what the clients were discussing. For the same reason, later he also studied the clients' preliminary thinking on the financial model, which ultimately would be core to the final China strategic plan.

Kees also proposed that the ground rules for the meeting should be explicit (see above, Strategic Dialogue Ground Rules). Given that the meeting team would have to work fast without the benefit of prepared data and analysis, he further proposed the lead ground rule would be "vigor over rigor". *This meant that the knowledge and judgment of all assembled on the team would be required and trusted.* There would be no time, nor need, during the 3 days for additional data and analysis. By making the ground rule explicit, Kees also contracted with the group that in his capacity as facilitator, he would champion vigor over rigor. If any managers were reluctant to proceed without more data, Kees would challenge them to trust their own judgment, knowledge and experience. He would remind them that in 3 days they could and would develop the framework for the China Growth strategy. During the following 90 days, there would be time to fill in the details with more data and analysis, as needed.

Ground rules
Vigor over rigor: concentrate on the big picture
Provide opportunities for everybody to speak up—try to understand the other person
Consultative Consensus decision making: differences in viewpoints are normal—listen to each other—if all clear, decide and move on. If no agreement—team leader provides direction
Say what you are really thinking and why you want things
Think in a much more entrepreneurial way than usual: China is a rapidly growing market with its own specific requirements.
Expect the Chinese culture to be very different. Be open to colleagues who have experience and ask their advice.
Agenda serves as guideline—modify timings as needed
Mutual commitment for timings: flag when discussions get too long or off track.
Shared breaks
Cell phones? Telephone breaks?

Participants and roles
The participants for the meeting were selected based on the criterion that those with the lead responsibility for the eventual implementation of the strategy across the various functions and geographies would collaboratively develop the strategy. With this in mind, the participants who were invited comprised:
Eighteen (18) people, including a balance of Chinese; British; Americans, Australians, Canadians and Swedes representing Sales/Marketing, Finance, IT, Operations, Human Resources, Supply Chain, Engineering, Quality and Human Resources. The Managing Director of the Eurasia region was not included, but did participate as one of the co-sponsors together with the two CEOs. The Managing Director was widely seen as supportive of the need to develop the China business rapidly, including making it independent of the Eurasia Region. Further, he was widely respected for his knowledge, expertise and contributions to the business.

MS would serve as the project leader and the ultimate decision maker in the room, when the consensus process required his intervention and Kees, a Dutchman, would serve as the facilitator of the process of the meeting dialogue.

In addition, the two sponsors, the CEOs of HMM and Q&I, and their two entire management teams would also join. Their collective role would be to sign off on the strategy and assure that all resources necessary would be made available. They would also serve as enablers of implementation. With all of their shared understanding and commitment all functional departments would be supportive. If and when roadblocks emerged and competing priorities would have to be resolved, the CEOs and members of their management teams would step in, as necessary. At the beginning of the meeting they would present the goals and scope of the exercise to the participants and entertain questions. And at the end of the meeting they would receive the proposal from the participants and act as ultimate decision makers.

Finally, in attendance would be the new future director of HMM China, a Chinese national, TS, who also had had considerable international business experience.

Venue
Beijing was selected by MJ for its symbolic value. He wanted to reinforce the message that aggressively growing the China business was a corporate priority.

Dates
Consistent with the sense of urgency which MJ had stressed, the strategy meeting was scheduled for the following month.

Communications to the participants in preparation for the meeting
Three weeks before the meeting the participants were invited. All of the issues which had been resolved in the preparatory meeting in Johannesburg were communicated. The overall message was clear. Senior management was fully committed to significant, accelerated growth of the China business. The meeting participants had the responsibility to develop the strategy creatively to get it done and later to be the leaders of its implementation. The urgency was unmistakable. They were being called upon to deliver one of the highest priorities of the corporation, globally, in a highly unconventional, ambitious and time limited fashion. The burden was being placed on their own know-how, expertise and drive. The stakes for the corporation and for each participant were extremely high. No doubt, never in the careers of any of the participants had they ever been expected to deliver outcomes of such significance through a single meeting.

The China Growth Strategy Meeting
January Year 2

The sponsors, project leader and facilitator were firm that the agenda for the strategy meeting, which had been so carefully prepared, would be followed meticulously with the support of the facilitator. If, along the way, modifications to the agenda would be required, then the project leader and facilitator would make those decisions since the sponsors would only be present for the introductory morning and for the presentation of the recommendations at the end of the meeting.

Day 1
8:00 AM
Sponsors and HMM and Q&I Management Teams: introduction to goals, objectives and scope

The presence of the entire management teams of the two divisions was intended to convey symbolically to all participants and the members of the management teams, as well, that this meeting was a corporate priority. They would remain for the entire morning. Questions and discussion were deferred until later in the morning. Every member of the two management teams was committed to the carefully developed goals, objectives and scope. There was no doubt that the full leadership of the corporation, including the CEO of the parent company, the boss of the CEOs of HMM and Q&I, strongly supported the urgent development and implementation of China growth strategy.

Personal Introductions

Many of the team members did not know each other. An implicit objective of the meeting would be the development of trusting relationships among the members who represented different functions and were located in different geographies around the world. These introductions would "break the ice'. Through working together the members would get to know each other more closely in terms of how they work and through the dinners they could also get to know each other more deeply personally.

Review Agenda, Process Overview and Ground Rules

The step of reviewing the agenda, the meeting process to be employed and the ground rules was intended to assure the participants that while the task was challenging, there was a method in which the leadership had confidence, by which they could achieve the task successfully. This was also an opportunity for participants to ask questions and make suggestions for modifications to assure their understanding, buy-in and commitment to the meeting, in all of its aspects. Nothing controversial was raised.

Hopes and Concerns

As a further step of engaging the participants a brainstorm exercise was conducted on what they considered to be their hopes and concerns for the meeting, including its purposes. This exercise was intended to stimulate the motivation of the participants to contribute to the meeting creatively, as well as to discover issues that needed to be addressed later in the agenda. Again, nothing controversial was raised. The anticipation to get to work was building.

Current Reality-A: Data sharing HMM and Q&I

Members of the two management teams presented baseline data on their current businesses in China including the market conditions. The intention was to establish an agreed fact-based starting point before proceeding to the development of the strategy. This step helped make the business case for the urgency of developing the China strategy.

Goals, objectives and scope—discussion

The participants were invited to be frank with their questions and challenges, if they had any, to the sponsors and the two top management teams. One significant point of contention arose: why focus only on the small market segment of top line products, their current market niche (see sidebar box, "In scope/ out of scope")? The questions and challenges indicated a significant level of anxiety to which one person gave voice: "you are asking us to go on a "mission impossible". MJ was able to respond to and counter every objection. The more he explained, the more the team understood his logic. They were persuaded that his argument was well informed and compelling. He was personally committed to the success of the China strategic plan which they would create; he was publicly putting his own reputation on the line. This point represented the first "healthy debate". The participants felt listened to, persuaded and educated. They also demonstrably conveyed confidence in and respect for their leader. While they were initially persuaded, as would be seen in the meeting, nonetheless for some of them, doubts remained and they were not yet fully committed.

1:30 PM
Current Reality-B: Identify key issues to be resolved

The team was ready to dive into the substance. Guided by the facilitator and informed by the current reality discussion, as well as their own knowledge, they engaged in a comprehensive, dynamic and rapid brainstorm to identify the key issues to resolve in the strategy development process. Vigorously employing the common place "SWOT" strategic framework they enumerated their strengths and weaknesses, as well as their threats and opportunities via a "story-board brainstorm" exercise. Within one hour they had brainstormed, categorized and prioritized the key components which they would need to develop in the preliminary version of their strategy over the next two days.

Desired State: Subgroup work to develop solutions

The project leader and facilitator had planned that solutions or components to the strategy would be developed by different subgroups working simultaneously, in parallel, on different, albeit related, functional topics, as explained above in the description of the preparatory meeting Johannesburg. As they anticipated, the participants raised several objections to the process. The anticipated critical juncture of the meeting had arrived. Some were skeptical that given the shortness of time in the meeting, that the individual functional solutions could ultimately be integrated if they worked in parallel. In addition, some continued to doubt that the strategy could be successful by focusing only on the top line, tier-one product segment. Next, the amount of time for the exercise, approximately two hours, seemed impossibly short to achieve complex and important outcomes, especially since many were tired due to jet lag. Finally, some felt a need for more guidance and input from senior management.

The project leader and facilitator patiently addressed all the concerns. The facilitator made sure that all objections were fully raised. First, they reviewed MJ's reasoning as to why the focus on top-line, tier-one products was essential. They also pointed out that MJ had made the decision. It was no longer negotiable. They also explained that given the parameters for the meeting as established by the sponsors that they had no choice but to take the risk and work in subgroups, simultaneously, in parallel on the different yet related topics. They gave feedback to the team on their performance to that point in the meeting in order to support the expectation that the exercise would succeed. They had been working collaboratively during the meeting in spite of their different perspectives; and they did share an understanding of the broad framework of what was expected. Next, while two hours would be too short to develop comprehensive plans as elements for the total strategy, the expectation was that this exercise would be a first iteration and two hours would be sufficient. The participants needed to remember that over the succeeding 90 days there would be time to flesh out the strategy in greater detail. They stressed the ground rule of "vigor" rather than "rigor" and the need to confidently tap into the respective knowledge and expertise of every participant in the room. Finally, for those who felt a need for more guidance, there were two Strawman documents which had been prepared by the facilitator and the project leader; one for the make or buy strategy and the other for the 5 year sales projections.

While the arguments were persuasive, not every participant was convinced. Ultimately, the project leader needed to invoke his decision making authority and instruct the participants to form the groups around the priority topics. As he later reported to Kees, this moment was frightening. He feared rebellion and needed to muster his courage to be directive. With continued hesitation by some, they all cooperated, or at least, complied. They assigned themselves to the priority solution areas which they had identified earlier, each of which would result in a preliminary plan: HR recruitment, manufacturing facilities, make-buy sourcing, 5 year marketing and sales, engineering intellectual property protection, creation of China as an independent business region within the HMM structure, and IT infrastructure.

The facilitator moved from group to group to support them in their process of working. He assured that each group had a moderator and a note taker. He coached them to work quickly, listen to one another and focus on points of agreement.

Joint sharing of draft solutions
The first day of work was concluded with brief reports from each of the subgroups. They had all come over the hump of resistance; clearly,

each group had been productive. The day concluded with a sense of accomplishment. Before going to dinner, the facilitator, the project leader and the subgroup leaders transcribed all the proposals into an edited and consistent format for in depth review the next morning.

Day 2
8:00 PM
Review of day 1 results
Each of the subgroups presented their draft solutions for their part of the strategic plan in detail to the full group. Each group demonstrated creativity, practicality and consistency with the clear goals set out by the sponsors. For example, the colleagues were impressed with the proposal from the sourcing make-buy strategy subgroup which described a distribution model including a distribution center. They also were impressed with the proposal from the manufacturing facilities subgroup to create two new factories, including prospective locations and manpower requirements. Progressively, it dawned upon the group that the China Growth strategic plan had now been fully established in broad strokes! They amazed themselves. Palpable, positive energy swept the group. The previous day's feeling of being on a "mission impossible", including resistance to work in subgroups and the anxiety expressed over the difficulty of succeeding with only tier 1, top line products flipped to a mood of high motivation and optimism. It was also recognized that not only would the China Growth strategy, when implemented, be boon to the HMM business, each individual also stood to gain. It was a career opportunity to be a part of designing and implementing a business of such scale and strategic import for the corporation.

While they recognized that the overall strategy still had gaps, they were confident that during the subsequent 90 days of further development and fine-tuning of the strategy, the gaps would be filled. Prominent on the agenda yet to be addressed were the following: What would be the required culture in the China business to cultivate to support the strategic plan? What organization design would be necessary? What would be the financial plan?

Desired state, continued: Further development of solutions, as needed
The subgroups reconvened to refine their draft solutions in consideration of what they heard from their colleagues in the other subgroups. The

interdependencies of the plans began to be addressed explicitly. They all recognized that the plans from the individual functions would need to be further integrated in order to create the final, holistic strategy. The integration would happen in iterations. During the meeting the head of Human Resources began to address the manpower and training which would be required. He began with what he called was a "rough cut" plan. During the meeting he met briefly with each of the other subgroups in order to get their feedback and enhance his rough cut plan. He would continue to consult with all the subgroups over the 90 day follow up period until the manpower and training plan was fully integrated with the needs of all of the functional departments.

Action planning
After a brief introduction to the action planning process and the overall project time lines by the facilitator and the project leader the subgroups convened once again. This time they worked on their 90 day action plans specifying how they would expand and substantiate their initial strategic solutions, as necessary. They were confident that while continuing to work within their functional areas that there would be sufficient points of communication among the subgroups, with the support of the project leader and facilitator that after 90 days they would have a fully integrated, robust and powerful China Growth strategic plan.

1:30 PM
Continued action plan development and large group sharing of action plans
The action planning culminated in another full group meeting in which each of the individual action plans was shared. The alignment which pleased everyone in the morning was further reinforced. They all also experienced the creative tension of working efficiently and quickly to prepare the final presentation to the sponsors and the top management teams of HMM and Q&I the next day.
The group discussion proceeded to the specifics of organizing and scheduling project follow-up activities, including preparation for the 30 and 60 day reviews and preparation of the final strategy at the end of 90 days. In addition, an overall communications plan was developed which was designed to inform all key stakeholders in the corporation as to their plans and progress. They agreed that the subgroup leaders, the project leader and the facilitator would have a weekly conference call

to monitor progress. In the disciplined spirit of the entire process, the conference calls would have specific agendas, key information would be shared, problems identified, potential solutions explored and careful notes taken and distributed.

Day 3
8:00 AM
Presentation dry run and final presentation adjustments
The subgroups met one final time to refine their presentations. And the full group met one more time to listen to the presentations of each subgroup. This was the dress rehearsal.

11:00 AM
Presentation to the Sponsors
The two sponsors, the CEOs of HMM and Q&I and their respective management teams returned to the proceedings. The presentations were presented confidently. All elements were accepted by the sponsors and their colleagues with only one exception. MJ required a more thorough analysis as quickly as possible regarding the make-buy strategy, i.e., which parts, sub-assemblies and components would be sourced externally and which would be made by HMM China. He was speaking to the sensitivity that all managers felt regarding the need to protect their intellectual property in a country famous for intellectual property abuses. Some managers on all levels had expressed doubts of manufacturing in China at all for this reason. MJ recognized that the doubts needed to be thoroughly addressed, both to protect the company, as well as to assure that his managers continued to support the strategy. He invited the sourcing sub-group which had worked on the make-buy strategy to meet with other key senior managers the next week to further develop the proposal and address detailed unanswered questions.

Given the number of sub-components to the overall strategy, the overall complexity and the high stakes, it was agreed that at 45 days there would be another two day meeting in Beijing to continue the planning process. All sub-groups would reconvene and with the benefit of being together the multiple points concerning integration of plans would be addressed. Another careful iteration to address the sensitive topic of intellectual property protection would also be on the agenda. Unanswered components of the strategy would also be addressed, including the financial strategy and details of the proposed IT infrastructure.

The meeting concluded on a note of optimism, excitement and pride in work well done. The motivation was high among all to continue the detailed strategic planning process over the coming 90 days to deliver a winning China Growth strategic plan.

Sponsors, team leader and facilitator debrief
The final activity of the conference was a review of the process and progress achieved in the meeting. These four individuals, the sponsors, the team leader and the facilitator had been the central team in designing and executing every step of the meeting process. They felt pleased with the progress and further committed to a disciplined process over the coming 90 days. The commitment remained high; as did the optimism that the process would yield a winning China Growth strategic plan.

The post-meeting 30-60-90 day process of detailed strategic planning
The momentum of the meeting was maintained throughout the succeeding days until the final presentation to senior management which was scheduled 90 days after the conclusion of the meeting. The follow up meeting on the sourcing make-buy strategy did occur in the week following the strategy meeting. The project and leader and the facilitator did maintain the weekly monitoring telephone conference calls with the subgroup leaders. The second meeting in Beijing was convened at the 45 day mark. Comprising two days the participants found working together in the same place enormously beneficial once again. Once again the group experienced the joy and amazement of how well the components of the strategy continued to fit together. The details of how the final strategy would be written were also planned. While the strategy would have ten authors, one for each component, it was agreed there would be one editor to assure a common style throughout.

Key challenges to complete the strategy in the next 45 days were also identified. The marketing and sales plan would still need to be verified by an independent marketing study. While this could not be done on time for the final presentation, the team felt confident that they could use sufficient other data to verify their assumptions and validate their 5 year sales projects. Their argument was persuasive and accepted by the sponsors. The financial strategy, including the payback and sensitivity analyses also still needed to be completed. While the details were not there, yet, the team was confident that the emergent financial strategy would justify the investments and the hopes for success in China and they would be able to complete their work in time. The facilitator also schooled himself in the details of the financial strategy since this would be fundamental to the final 90 day presentation to senior management and he would be facilitating that interaction.

The deadlines were met by all subgroups. The editor received all the component strategies on time so that the final edit resulted in a well written document with a consistent style. The team continued to execute with discipline.

Throughout the entire 90 day period, the meeting teams proactively involved senior management to assure their commitment and tap into their knowledge and expertise. The global finance head became involved in the financial strategy. The global engineering director became immersed in the intellectual property questions. In addition, MJ reviewed updates on the progress during the 90 days at each of his own senior management meetings. His support and commitment during the follow up period was demonstrable to all.

Finally, the 90 day presentation to the sponsors and their management teams was about to convene. The meeting teams met two days in advance. They cross referenced the financial strategy with all the component strategies and confirmed its soundness. They edited various points; integrated elements across the components; and also had a full dress rehearsal. On the third day, the meeting subgroup leaders presented their China Growth strategic plan. The intense work of 19 managers over the course of 90 days was vindicated. The sponsors accepted the plan and approved the funds. As of this writing, the implementation has gone well and financial targets are being met.

The Principles of Organizational Transformation and the case of accelerated strategy development

The accelerated strategy development process was grounded in trusting relationships. The CEO, MJ, had decided that his company, HHM, Inc.

needed to aggressively penetrate China and he trusted his own managers to develop the strategy rather than hire an external consultancy to do so. He knew that they knew the business, the capabilities of their own departments and the market. He also believed that if they did the strategy development they could do it much faster than any outside consultancy and in so doing, they would understand it, own it and implement it well. And he would save the expense of hiring an outside strategy consultancy. He also trusted Kees Bultink to be the facilitator of the process since they had worked together over the years on several meetings in which important, complex business problems were solved while utilizing the same meeting methodology intended for the development of the China strategic plan. As the preparation and the meeting, itself unfolded, the managers who were participants also strengthened their trust in one another based on the success they experienced in exceeding their own expectations in developing the framework of a strategy in such a short period of time—a 2.5 day meeting.

Kees supported the process across all three time scales: the moments, meetings and the macro process. The team did achieved the "ah ha" moment of shared awareness when they found that the individual functional strategies all fit together coherently, as Kees had argued they would. He also facilitated the entire meeting step by step through the carefully designed agenda, as well as the preparatory meeting in Johannesburg. And finally, Kees facilitated the overall macro process over the succeeding 90 days during which the strategy was finalized and formally proposed to MJ and his senior management team for budgeting. The entire process—the preparation, the meeting and the following 90 days were all characterized by the process of dialogue to mobilize commitment. While there was some resistance from some of the participants to participate, the power and influence of the CEO brought all the key managers to the table to work together. And they succeeded; the dialogue did result in a strategic plan with commitment from all who created it.

The meeting also employed the ground rules for strategic dialogue with a focus on Consultative Consensus decision making. The meeting also illustrated how barriers to dialogue due to different perceptions/ different realities were overcome. Each individual, representing different functions and different geographies had a voice. The dialogue resulted in the differences being reconciled and one plan being agreed by all. The participants learned a new approach to strategic planning by doing it; they experienced action learning.

The process also illustrated how clearly the boundaries of dialogue were defined and roles were clarified through the application of the principle of freedom within a framework. The conclusion of the 2.5 day meeting resulted in a framework for a strategic plan. Over the succeeding 90 days, more details were developed by the participants and other managers with knowledge and expertise. A specific example of the application was MJ's response to the proposals he received at the end of the meeting when he called the meeting on the sensitive intellectual property questions for the following week. For this meeting he invited members of his own senior management team.

By developing the strategy with internal managers who were ultimately responsible for its implementation, the goals of the transformation were achieved: a plan to leverage the resources of the company to penetrate the China market while strengthening the capability of the individual participants both in developing as well as in implementing that strategy. Only together could they develop and implement a complete strategy for China. By having all the key functions represented, the full scope of the organization as a system was included in the strategic plan. In recognition that all sub-systems interact with one another, the CEO, MJ, invited his counterpart, the CEO of the sister company, Q&I, to participate in the strategy development process, since whatever HMM developed as a strategy in China would have implications of Q&I's business in China, as well.

Chapter 14
Merger Integration
Facilitating meetings employing strategic and relational dialogue

Introduction

In leading a comprehensive organization transformation, once the leadership team has defined the parameters of the operating framework the next challenge is to mobilize the rest of the organization to share understanding, buy-in and commit to its implementation. As illustrated in Case I and II, the leadership team employs at least four approaches aimed at mobilizing the wider organization for the transformation: continued development of the leadership team in its effectiveness; a leadership conference with the top several levels of management; departmental meetings led by individual members of the leadership team; and interface meetings with two or more departments or divisions whose work is highly interdependent. This case will focus on the leadership conference as another case example of facilitating dialogue in an organizational transformation meeting. It will also highlight, once again, how meetings which are grounded in dialogue can play a pivotal role in the transformation process, just as our three previous cases had demonstrated.

The company in question, Euro Corporation, had acquired ABC. The merger integration had proceeded with growing doubts by ABC management that the integration could work effectively. Over the initial 6 months after the signing of the acquisition, the Euro Corp CEO had not advanced the design of the merged entity, nor had he engaged ABC management in questions regarding the future. This resulted finally in the alienation and the threatened resignation of the entire Leadership Team of ABC.

The Board of Directors of Euro Corp recognized they had a crisis. If ABC's management were to have departed they believed that the merger would have failed and they then would have lost the considerable investment they had made in the acquisition. They were acutely aware that the value of ABC resided significantly in the leadership of the Leadership Team and the relationships with multiple wine and spirits suppliers which they had developed over the years.

The Board of Directors of Euro Corp tried to save the merger and replaced the existing CEO with Mary who assumed her new position on June 1. While she had already been named to become the CEO and take the position some months later, she had been working with Euro Corp for some months. The Board had decided that they needed her to assume leadership earlier than planned in view of the deepening crisis.

In response to the Board of Director's anxiety, Mary committed to present to them an initial transformation plan and top line organizational structure within ten days of her appointment. She decided that she needed consultant assistance in order to move so quickly. She called Genesis whom she had known from previous work.

I was able to make myself available on short notice and commenced working with Mary immediately. Within one week of their first meeting, they planned and executed a meeting with members of the existing Leadership Teams of Euro Corp and ABC in order to develop the proposal for the Board: the initial transformation plan and organizational structure for the Board, including appointments to the new leadership team. Employing the Genesis Urgent Vision model as the basis for creating the operating framework for the new Euro Corp, they achieved consensus. In so doing they also honestly confronted the problems of the past six months and the failure to have previously achieved trust between the two teams. A spirit of collaboration and optimism emerged. The threat of the resignation of ABC managers evaporated.

The day after the meeting, Mary invited selected members of the two teams to fill the positions of the new leadership team which together they had designed. Everyone accepted. The Board ratified Mary's proposals. The crisis was past.

With the success of the first meeting, Mary asked me to continue working with her and her new leadership team. Over the next several months, they held two more leadership team meetings to define the parameters of the operating framework and more fully develop the transformation plan for the new Euro Corp. At the same time they continued to build themselves as a team and work to overcome the mistrust which had emerged between ABC and Euro Corp managers during the period before Mary became CEO.

By their own assessment they made significant progress. They summarized their work as a new leadership team at the end of their first meeting:
"As we continue with the merger integration and transformation process of the new Euro Corp., we have made the Euro Corp. (organization structure) matrix workable by defining the key processes and clarifying the roles and responsibilities within the leadership team. We also deepened our teamwork. This was the next decisive step of the integration process."
They also agreed that the message for the employees during these early days of the new organization would be "business as usual—keep on delivering". They would communicate more of the details of the new organization and operating framework only after they had defined it all more completely themselves.

They summarized their work after the second meeting which occurred six weeks later:
"We have reviewed and deepened all elements of the operating framework: the business model, values, processes and structure. We also have begun to address some of our more difficult operational challenges."

Operational challenges identified and addressed early by the new Leadership Team

As a European region company they had contracts with many suppliers of wines and spirits. Some were regional, some national and some sub-regional within a country. Many suppliers competed with one another. How would Euro Corp grow their relationships with suppliers and manage the competition among the suppliers?

With the acquisition of ABC, Euro Corp also acquired its subsidiary, LOGI, a logistics company. Given that logistics is a critical component of the value proposition of a distribution company, ABC had created its own logistics company to control this aspect of the value chain. In order to increase volumes, operating efficiencies and economies of scale, LOGI also sold its services to distributors other than ABC, itself. Over the years the ABC managers found that LOGI had become a distraction and a financial burden, as profitability was difficult to attain and the total set of logistics processes and competencies was a different business from the marketing and selling of wines and spirits, where Euro Corp. felt it had to concentrate. Euro Corp. inherited the problem and Mary quickly became open to the notion that LOGI should be divested; while recognizing the necessity of quality logistics to the emerging business model of Euro Corp. The emerging solution would be to sell off LOGI while retaining roles and competencies within Euro Corp to manage the interface with the external logistics partner.

The team unanimously decided to divest LOGI and assigned the task of developing the divestiture plan to the head of manufacturing.

The Leadership Team's summary of their work continued: "We have also deepened our trusting relationships with one another."

Story telling as team building

As a setting for the Leadership Team to further their develop their relationships with one another, as the meeting was held in Lapland at the end of August

The site was a field near the river, filled with low lying plants festooned with ripe blueberries, surrounded by birches and conifers. The evening sun hovered for hours, even as the days of summer were waning. Before dinner, wine was shared by all and each team member was invited to tell their personal story.

The stories became intimate revelations including troubled marriages, difficult youths and ultimately, later in the evening, back in the cabin, the grief still felt for parents who had died in recent years. The intimacy had a transformative impact on the team; the increased trust was almost palpable. In a the course of three two day meetings, the managers of ABC and Euro Corp who had almost failed to merge their two businesses after the acquisition was signed nine months earlier were now gelling as a team.

At least one member acknowledged nearly one year later that through these exchanges he discovered in himself emotions and values that, until then, had been outside his immediate awareness. Concomitantly Mary and I and other members of the Leadership Team felt that his effectiveness as a leader had also strengthened.

The Leadership Conference

The Leadership Team had begun the planning of a Leadership Conference with the next level managers (i.e., direct reports of the Leadership Team plus selected others) at their second meeting in Lapland. In their summary of that meeting they agreed on the goals of the Leadership Conference:

"We are now ready to communicate, modify as needed and validate our work with our next level managers and work with them to fill in the details with an intensive leadership conference." Through dialogue, the participants would share understanding, buy-in and be committed to the new Euro Corp organization

They also acknowledged that the Leadership Conference would be one more opportunity for the Leadership Team to strengthen their leadership of the business as one Leadership Team. It would be important that they would communicate their plans for the new Euro Corp with "one voice".

They gave themselves an aggressive lead time of only three weeks. The Leadership Conference would begin mid-day on 20. September and conclude mid-day on 23. September. This would comprise three full days of work, including three evenings for relationship building.

Preparation

Mary and I developed the first draft of the detailed agenda based on the outline agreed with the Leadership Team.

Given that the total number of participants would number 70, Mary agreed that Genesis would provide an additional three facilitators.

Genesis consultants also met one on one with individual Leadership Team members to review and plan the details of the segments of the agenda that pertained to their areas. This allowed the Genesis consultants who were new to Euro Corp to become familiar the culture and for the Leadership Team members to begin to cultivate working partnership with the consultants with whom they would be working.

The Leadership Team and the Genesis consultants also met together to review the entire agenda, the processes to be employed and the roles that everyone would play in the meeting.

Methodology

The meeting would allocate significant time to dialogue. While the Leadership Team had reached conclusions about the vision for the new Euro Corp organization, including its business model, values, processes and structure, they would invite their next level colleagues to "add to, amend and validate" their work. In addition they would also develop greater detail and specificity with their colleagues in the various aspects of the new organization. This approach would faciliate the process by which the participates would gain understanding and develop buy-in and commitment to the new organization.

Explicitly, Mary would introduce the meeting with an overview of the new Euro Corp organization and invitation to all the participants to exercise their own freedom within the framework to be presented by the Leadership Team. The Genesis facilitators would facilitate the sub-group discussions to support this process.

The Leadership Team anticipated one especially difficult challenge in the new organization whereby next level manager would be expected and required to shift from a history of internal competition to a future of collaboration in certain areas of work while maintaining competition in the traditional areas. A simulation exercise was planned so the participants could experience how they would manage this paradox of combining competition and collaboration in their relationships with one another.

A challenge of shifting from internal competition to collaboration

In the prior ABC organization within each Euro Corp region country "company managing directors" ran different "companies" with different company names all under the the umbrella of ABC. They functioned as competitors only since they represented different suppliers who wanted distributors dedicated to their own interests exclusively. In the new Euro Corp structure the company managing directors would report to the SVP of the country, a new role, and while they would be expected to continue to compete in terms of representing their respective suppliers they would now also be expected to collaborate in selling to the largest customers. The potential for sales growth through the collaboration of the companies within a country was easy to envision—in a single transaction with Euro Corp one customer could purchase a variety of wines and spirits from different suppliers as a total solution. Yet changing the behavior and mindset of the company managing directors would not be easy, the Leadership Team anticipated, since they had been competing with one another for years and their suppliers had grown accustomed to having distributors (the former ABC companies) fully dedicated to their own interests only.

Groundrules

The Leadership Team agreed to employ the same groundrules which they had used in their own meetings, i.e., the Genesis groundrules.

Euro Corp. Leadership Conference
Ground-rules for Dialogue, Healthy Debate and Decision making

- **_Listen_**
  Probing questions
  Paraphrasing
  Building comments on what others have said
  One conversation at a time

- **_Express your views_**
  Dialogue and Debate openly/ honestly
  No sacred cows
  Spotlight on the difficult issues where people disagree
  All debates are team debates; encourage the views of everyone and stop repetitious debates

- **_Bring Underlying Assumptions to the table_**
  recognize that we each view Altia with different perspectives or mental models which shape our perceptions. Ask Why? Why? Why?

- **_Respect each individual_**
  No hierarchy in the dialogue; all opinions are considered; during the dialogue any opinion by anyone may be disagreed with; No personal attacks; No hostile sarcasm

- **_Accept that different people are at different stages of understanding, buying in and committing to the new Altia_**

- **_Manage the timings flexibly and punctually_**—shared breaks

- Other...

Euro Corp
20-23 September
Kick-off of the New Euro Corp Organization

Day I
20. September/ Tuesday
13:00

Welcome and Purpose

The CEO, Mary, opened the meeting with a hearty welcome and a brief overview of the work done by the Leadership Team to design the newly merged Euro Corp. She explained that the Leadership Conference would be devoted to a high degree of dialogue on all aspects of the new organization. While the Leadership Team had taken some key decisions on the broad framework of the organization, there would be freedom within the framework for all of the participants to question, challenge and, if agreed by the Leadership Team, modify the framework. She explained that after the Leadership Conference work of this week, within every Leadership Team and department, the work done here would be reviewed and the details would continue to be designed as needed and implemented. She encouraged patience and expected that not everyone would understand and buy-in at the same time. Through dialogue, she emphasized, it would be important to respect the different views and over time seek consensus across the entire Euro Corp organization.

Framework for the new Euro Corp

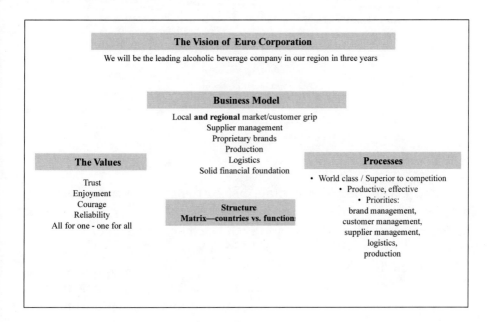

The Vision of Euro Corporation
We will be the leading alcoholic beverage company in our region in three years

Business Model
Local **and regional** market/customer grip
Supplier management
Proprietary brands
Production
Logistics
Solid financial foundation

The Values
Trust
Enjoyment
Courage
Reliability
All for one - one for all

Structure
Matrix—countries vs. functions

Processes
• World class / Superior to competition
• Productive, effective
• Priorities:
brand management,
customer management,
supplier management,
logistics,
production

Purpose of the Leadership Conference

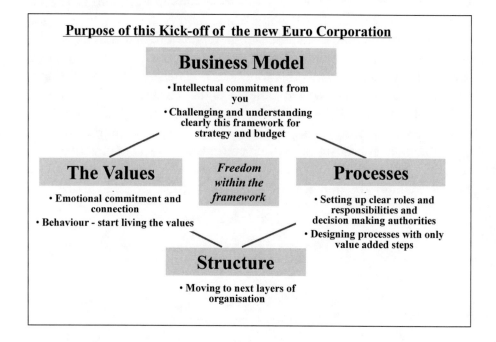

Hopes and Concerns

Consistent with the Genesis philosophy of engaging participants in a meeting the next activity was a brainstorm of the hopes and concerns that the participants had both for the Leadership Conference and more generally for the creation of the new Euro Corp based on the merger with ABC. Given that this was the first opportunity that managers from the two former separate companies met, the exercise was organized in small groups of six people ("table teams") with a mix of people from both companies. The table teams were given twenty minutes to brainstorm and determine their top three hopes and top three concerns. A spokes person from each team then reported back to the plenary and the reports were recorded on a computer which was attached to a projector so everyone could simultaneously listen and read the individual reports.

The candor was revealing. The major themes addressed the challenges that the differences represented by the two merged companies, Euro Corp from Country X and ABC from Country Y. It was evident right at the beginning of the meeting that even though the Leadership Team comprising managers from both Euro Corp and ABC had made significant progress in finding common ground in the past few months through their own meetings, the challenge would be significant for the next level managers to do the same. This conference would be the first major opportunity to address the differences and begin to close the gaps by giving all the participants' time to build relationships with one another, while working in designing the details of their new organization.

Hopes and Concerns highlights

The following differences were emphasized as presenting challenges to the merger:

- One country culture is faster on decision making and shorter on communication than the second country culture. The third culture is in between.
- Euro Corp has been owned by one national government and has been bureaucratic while ABC has been independently owned and has been entrepreneurial
- Euro Corp has had a tradition of being one company while ABC has been an assemblage of a group of small companies, each one dedicated to its own suppliers and in competition with one another.
- Euro Corp has its own proprietary brands and ABC has only brands from a vast array of different suppliers. Clarifying our relationships with suppliers, including roles and responsibilities is a high priority.

Ground rules and agenda review
On behalf of the Leadership Team and the Genesis consultants, I then introduced the proposed ground rules and the agenda and solicited questions or suggestions. Once again, the aim was to encourage shared understanding, buy-in and commitment among all the participants.

The Transformation Process so far
In order to create context for the meeting, one of the members of the Leadership Team presented a brief overview of the work the new Leadership Team had done in designing the new Euro Corp in its three prior meetings. Candidly, he mentioned that the process of bringing together the senior managers from the two companies to forge the new Leadership Team had also been a journey from suspicion to the beginnings of trust.

Vision, Sustainable Business Model, Structure
Three closely related aspects of the core of the new Euro Corp framework
were next presented by two more members of the Leadership Team, one
a former ABC manager and the other a former Euro Corp manager. It
was decided by the Leadership Team that having one manager from each
of the former companies make the presentation would symbolically
convey that the managers from the former companies had come to
shared understanding on the critical questions:
Vision—where are we going?
Sustainable business model—how do we make money; and how do we
compete?
Structure—how are we organized?

Next, the participants were divided into four working groups comprising
a mix of former ABC and old-Euro Corp managers, including members
of the Leadership Team and facilitated by a Genesis consultant. To
assure as open and full a dialogue as possible the process was designed
in advance and reviewed together by the Leadership Team members and
the consultants. It comprised the following:
Since each working group would have almost twenty participants, the
working session would begin with groups of 3 or 4. Each small group
was asked to comment on the presentation:
What struck you, what impressed you, how are we different from the
competition?
Each small group reported back to the plenary and the comments were
recorded electronically by the consultant.
Next, the full group was encouraged to pose questions to the Leadership
Team members who were present and the Leadership Team members
were expected to answer the questions.
Next, the full group was encouraged to present any challenges or doubts
that they had.
Finally, the group was guided to validate those elements on which
everyone could agree.
The highlights of the entire conversation were recorded electronically
by the consultant.

At the end of the hour, the participants were given a break while the
Leadership Team members and their partner consultant prepared a
synthesis report to be presented back to the fully plenary after thirty

minutes. The emphasis would be to highlight key outstanding challenges and questions. If necessary, additional answers would be provided in the plenary by Mary and the full Leadership team.

Vision, Sustainable Business Model, Structure

Feedback from the working groups

Each of the groups presented multiple points, including elements they heard which inspired them (positive) and elements which confused or troubled them (concerns). The following is a list of representative comments which later emerged as recurrent themes for the company to grapple with.

Positive points

- The new structure included each country with its member companies.
- This would enable greater coordination across the various markets within a country.
- The process of this Leadership Conference involves all of us significantly. Each of us has a voice!
- The vision of becoming the leading pan-Euro region wine and spirits company is exciting and attainable; we have presence in all the markets and a broad portfolio; yet it must be specified in greater detail

Concerns

- How can we maintain the historic success of our unique and independent companies, now that they are tightly subsumed within the country structure?
- How will the matrix decision making work between central functions such as finance and supplier management and the individual countries and their member companies?
- How will we reassure suppliers that this new structure is in their interest and the dedication they enjoyed in the past will not become diluted?
- How will we maintain our core competence in logistics if and when we divest our logistics company, LOGI?

Response from Mary

- Yes, the Leadership Team will develop the vision more precisely based on the input you have given
- The concerns will all be addressed as we continue to work together in the coming months in filling in the details of our operating framework.
- We also have several more days of work here together.
- We will maintain our core competence in logistics, even when we divest LOGI, since we still must maintain expert roles to guide and interface with any new external logistics partner.

Inspiring Values and Culture

The values were next presented by another member of the Leadership Team in greater detail than Mary's introduction in the morning. Concrete examples were also presented by different members of the Leadership Team in order to both illustrate the values in action and further demonstrate the alignment of the Leadership Team.

Working groups were then convened in the plenary hall ("table teams") to discuss the values and prepare comments back to the plenary. The groups were asked to consider the following questions:
How do we make these values real in every day behavior with?
What expectations do we have of the Leadership Team and ourselves?
What further actual examples of the values in action?
Are there values missing which you feel passionately should be included?

Euro Corp Values	
Trust	**Responsibility**
We	We are responsible, accountable
Keep our promises	and caring toward
Maintain integrity	Consumers of alcohol
Respect each individual and	Our people
diversity	Our customers
	Our suppliers
	Our environment

Enjoyment We Create a relaxed atmosphere to help achieve results Are both casual and professional Find fun in winning, being dedicated and feeling we belong	**All for one—one for all** We Are interdependent, aligned in our vision and values and pull the rope together to win Leverage our resources Become stronger as individuals, teams and units by being part of the total Euro Corp Corporation Practice teamwork Are dedicated and committed
Courage We Are entrepreneurial Play to win Challenge each other's ideas and behaviors to become better continuously (give feedback) Take appropriate risks Exercise freedom within the Euro Corp framework	

While the presentations were received with apparent interest and laughter at humorous examples and the table teams were animated, the presentations by the table teams back to the plenary were abbreviated. Perhaps this was due to the typical difficulty which business people have in discussing values in depth—rather than business—and/or because it was late in the day and energy was beginning to run low.

Getting acquainted

The plenary for the day concluded with an invitation, in the time before dinner, to form groups of three with people one did not know in order to get acquainted. The participants were encouraged to consider the following talking points:

Tell your story of your experience of the merger integration the past 9 months after the acquisition of ABC by Euro Corp was finalized.

Tell your personal story and highlight your personal values

Choose your venue: walk outside? Have a sauna? Other?

Leadership Team feedback on the day

While the participants were meeting with one another the Leadership Team and the Genesis Consultants convened to review and assess the day. How did the process work? What were the most important content issues which arose? The Leadership Team felt quite positive about the level of enthusiastic engagement by the participants during the day. The process of dialogue seemed effective. The concerns which had been raised, it was felt, would all be addressed over the coming days of the Leadership Conference and certainly in the weeks and months to follow as the new participants lived the new Euro Corporation. The team made no changes to the agenda.

The evening

The aim for the evening was for the participants to get to know each other better. At the conclusion of the working session, they were encouraged to form teams of three who did not know each other previously and spend an hour together. The activity would be unstructured. The goal would simply be for participants to learn more about one another, particularly on a personal basis. The dinner would also be informal, with the same goal.

Day II
21. September/ Wednesday
8:30

21. September / Wednesday

Reflections on Day I; Agenda Review

The conference re-convened with an invitation by myself as facilitator for anyone to comment on Day I—what worked well? What could have been improved? Are there outstanding issues? No one offered any significant challenges or controversial comments. The mood appeared to the Genesis consultants as one of positive engagement and anticipation of the next steps of the agenda. The agenda was reviewed without questions or suggestions for modification.

Strategy Process overview

The VP of Business Development, a member of the Leadership Team, and formerly, the CEO of the acquired company, ABC, briefly presented how he would lead a business strategy development process over the coming months which involve all the managers in the conference plus others, as well.

Budgeting Process overview
The VP of Finance, also a member of the Leadership Team briefly presented how the output of the Strategy Process would be input to the Budgeting Process and how the Budgeting Process would unfold over the coming months.

Strategy Process is kicked off: the SWOT
The VP of Business Development then introduced a strategy exercise which explained would build on the business model and result in determining the product/market priorities for the business and the competencies required to realize them. He continued by introducing a Draft SWOT which the Leadership Team had developed and would serve as a catalyst for further discussion and modification, as needed. The acronym SWOT represents "strengths, weaknesses, opportunities and threats". (The SWOT is a widely used, robust strategy tool used by many companies.) The exercise would identify priority core competencies which needed to be further developed based on the SWOT, particularly the opportunities, weaknesses and threats. The strengths would be considered competencies already present and not in need of further identification at this time. The participants would work in the table teams in the conference room, again with a mix of geographies and functions and they would be asked to contribute answers to the following questions:
What are the priority opportunities? What are the associated core competencies?
What are the priority threats? What are the associated core competencies?
What are the priority weaknesses? What are the associated competencies?

Since this exercise was principally a brainstorming and prioritizing exercise and time was relatively short, as the facilitator, I guided the exercise. I explained that the goal was to optimize the contributions of everyone in the room in a short period of time. I allocated fifteen minutes to each pair of questions; instructed the table teams to solicit a volunteer discussion leader and a note taker at the outset; and emphasized that in each round the table teams should record their top 3-5 ideas, at the discretion of the discussion leader and note taker. I explained this was a time to settle on points of agreement and there was no time for debate on the points which were in disagreement. To assure that all the teams were working in parallel, I monitored the time-keeping rigorously from question to question.

At the end of each pair of questions I then solicited reports from each of the table teams and the input was recorded electronically and projected so that everyone could also read the ideas which were contributed. The Core Competencies for each question were copied to one sheet so that everyone could visualize the total set at one time. And finally, the plenary assigned votes to the core competencies in each area to see which priorities emerged (see chart, below, "Core Competencies").

CORE COMPETENCIES
to further develop which are difficult for competitors to copy and create significant value for our customers and suppliers

Core Competencies from opportunities	Core Competencies from threats	Core Competencies from weaknesses
1) Market knowledge--15	1. Logistic solutions--20	1. excellent...
2) Product dev--8		2. good leadership --16
3) Own brands pan-Nordic--15	2. understand the needs of the Suppliers--8	3. Understand the business and prioritize well; eye on the ball--18
4) Altia Academy/training--2	3. be present with suppliers--3	
5) Strong balance sheet--15		
6) Right people/right places--20	4. post merger integration- -3	4.Communication and clear targets--
	5. Sales org/ people--7	5.Personal relationship with our suppliers--14
7) Excellent production facilities--10	6. Strong Nordic brand teams-people--4	6.Best practice marketing and sales- -2
	7. Teamwork--14	7.Sell like hell--3
	8. Efficiency in brand execution--	
	9. Accurate target setting--	
	10. Understanding the Danish market--	

Reflection on the Content
The output of the strategy exercise revealed a recapitulation of the priority concern on Day I—logistics—in the exercise regarding the Vision, Business Model and Structure. It was now voted as a top priority core competence. Since the Leadership Team had announced

their decision to divest the logistics company, LOGI, the assembled managers remain concerned how they would continue to assure quality logistics as a service to their suppliers and to their customers. They all recognized that logistics excellence was essential to their success as a company. Their distribution patterns were highly complex and needed to be managed well in order to prevent bottlenecks, mistakes, financial losses and dissatisfied suppliers and customers.

Introduction of New Departments: Proprietary Brand Management and Supplier Brand Management

The new structure of Euro Corp, as a merged entity, would include two new departments: Proprietary Brand Management and Supplier Brand Management. The Vice Presidents of these two new departments introduced their missions and staff. Proprietary Brand Management would have the responsibility of marketing brands across all geographies which had been predominantly available only on the national market before the merger, when Euro Corp was only a national company. Supplier Brand Management would have the responsibility of leveraging brands from suppliers to be marketed in ever wider geographies across the entire region. Both departments were emblematic of significant changes in mindset, roles and decision making which would be required for them to be successful.

Exercise: Who has what role and decision authority within the processes?

In recognition of the need to clarify roles and decision making authorities in the new structure and consistent with the principle, "freedom within the framework" which the CEO had embraced and enunciated in her introduction to the conference, the next exercise would engage all participants to help design the details. The Leadership Team had anticipated correctly the processes which would need the most work and would be of greatest concern to the participants:
Supplier Management Process
Logistics
Brand Management, comprising Prorietary and Supplier Brand Management, as well as Market Intelligence
Management Accounting, Controlling and Decision Support

Each process already had a schematic, draft document, called a decision grid prepared in advance by the Leadership Team during their meetings. This would serve as a catalyst for discussion and a draft to be modified, as needed. Given the detailed work required, a full three hours was devoted to the task. Working teams were constituted with individuals who had the most involvement and knowledge of the business process in question. Since the decision grid tool would be new to most participants, the consultants facilitated each of the sessions. The final activity of the day was a reporting session from each of the working groups.

Leadership Team: feedback on the day
The Leadership Team reported that the exercise on roles and decision making authorities revealed the complexity of the challenge they faced in building their new organizations. While the participants appreciated the exercise and made progress, there remained a widely shared opinion that more work would be required in order to clearly implement the new roles and decision authorities of their new organization. For the former ABC managers the transformation would be great to shift from operating principally within individual companies, within countries which were dedicated to their own suppliers to greater collaboration among companies within countries, especially with respect to larger suppliers. For the former National Euro Corp managers, the transformation would be great to shift from operating only within Country X to now managing across the entire European region.

Dinner surprise
The objective of each evening's activity was to encourage relationship development and team building. This dinner began with an elaborate wine tasting contest. As a wine and spirits company, Euro Corp had a vast variety of fine wines in its portfolio and wine experts on staff, as well. The experts conducted a blind wine tasting and recognition contest. The participants were divided into teams who tasted the variety of wines available. They were then asked to identify what they had tasted. The team who was most correct received some bottles of fine wine as a prize.

To foster collaborative team work, the next phase of the dinner entailed cooking together. A professional catering company was hired who set up various cooking stations. Each station was focused on another course and was manned by a chef who had all the requisite food stuffs with which to prepare the course. Again the participants were divided into teams and each team was assigned to a station where together with the chef they prepared their course. When the preparations were completed everyone enjoyed the fruits of their labor.

Day III
22. September/ Thursday
8:30

Reflections on Day II
Once again the day began with a plenary session. The facilitator invited any reflections on day I and reviewed the agenda for the day, soliciting suggestions or modifications. The agenda was accepted, as is.

Country Team Meetings—competitive simulation
The first activity of the day would be a focus on how the new Euro Corp would serve major customers in each of the countries. In order for the participants, principally marketing managers, to experience the challenge rather than simply discuss it theoretically, the exercise selected was a simulation. The three largest countries in business volume in the group, Country X, Country Z and Country Y, would each form a working team comprising managers who worked in those countries. These country organizations also were complex in that they each comprised multiple smaller Euro Corp companies who were dedicated to serving different suppliers. They were each presented with the same Business Challenge; the objective was to create a sales plan designed to persuade a fictitious customer, a restaurant chain, to do business with Euro Corp. What would be the offer in terms of products and brands and what would be the terms and conditions, including logistics, service, pricing and payment? Each team would present their plan back to the plenary, again as a competition. The plenary participants would then vote on the most compelling plan as the winner.

The simulation was intended to address, experientially, the challenge for all managers in Euro Corp to begin to operate in a new way. After the merger they all now had a much broader product and brand portfolio to offer customers and accordingly, much greater complexity, including the challenge of managing the competitive attitude between and among suppliers.

Two country teams produced dynamic plans with relative ease. The third country team got bogged down in debates and found difficulty in agreeing on a collaborative plan. The SVP was concerned. The presentations from the three country teams were judged by the Logistics Team members for their dynamism and persuasiveness and the winning team members were awarded a bottle of wine each. The two country teams were almost tied for the most votes and the third team received almost no votes at all.

As was discussed later, at the end of the day by the Leadership Team, the difficulties were attributed to the Country Y business history. Country Y had been the principle country of operation for ABC (which had been acquired by Euro Corp). The managers in that country had managed their separate companies individually, with "firewalls" between them in order to assure their partners, the suppliers, would receive dedicated service. ABC had made it policy that suppliers would work with one company within ABC who would be devoted to serving their interests. The paradigm of the new Euro Corp was different—the largest suppliers would no longer be served only by one company, but rather by all the companies operating in a country. The Country Y managers would need to change more than their colleagues in the other countries.

Note: Flash forward—the meeting is not necessarily a predictor of actions which follow.
Months later, ironically, it was the third country team who actually did collaborate vis a vis certain restaurant chains and expanded their business while the two country teams still had not applied their success with the simulation to real business in a comparable fashion. Many factors during the follow up are the keys to success or failure. One factor, the SVP of Country Y later aknowledged, was that he had become persuaded that he could help grow his business with this collaborative approach, even though his team had not been ready for it at the Leadership Conference. Over time, he guided them to collaborate.

Logistics Team Action Planning
In parallel with the three simulations, a fourth working group was convened which focused on Logistics and the development of an action

plan to begin to prepare for the divestiture. The exercise, attended by the key logistics managers, was intended to commence a process of careful action planning to assure that the complex process of continuing to provide logistics support to suppliers and customers would be maintained while at the same time preparing the divestiture. The need for this exercise had been confirmed several times already in the meeting through the raising of concerns about the divestiture.

Note: flash forward—another example—the meeting is not necessarily a predictor of actions which follow.
Nearly one year later, the divestiture of Euro Corp's logistics company had still not occurred, even though the Leadership Team had been unanimous in deciding on the divestiture and in spite of the attention the question received at the Leadership Conference. The Leadership Team SVP who had led the process and his working team had developed doubts about the feasibility and desirability of the divestment. He had not shared those doubts with the CEO and the CEO, given other priorities, for all of those months had not followed up to monitor progress on the divestment.

Supplier Management Simulation—action plans for a representative supplier
Another new area of collaboration would be the opportunity to develop relationships with major suppliers; i.e., suppliers who were large enough to be interested in selling their wines and spirits in multiple countries in which Euro Corp was present. Once again, the aim was for participants to begin to learn to work in this new, collaborative fashion through the experience of a simulation. Participants were divided into three heterogeneous teams which mixed country of origin, as well as organizational function. All the teams were given the same general description of a fictitious major supplier and the assignment to develop a presentation to the supplier as part of an approach to win the supplier as a business partner who would sell their wines and spirits through Euro Corp to the European region markets. The teams would make their completed presentations to the full plenary at the end of the afternoon. Once again, colleagues who were not in the working teams would serve as judges and determine which team had the winning presentation. And once again, the winners of the competition would be awarded one bottle of wine for each team member.

Proprietary Brand Management Action Plan
At the same time as the supplier management simulation was occurring, in parallel, the actual members of the Proprietary Brand Leadership Team gathered for a real meeting. Given the newness of the organization, the team had not yet been able to complete an action plan of how they would proceed in their new roles in their new team. They were now given the opportunity to do so. After they completed their working session, they, too, made a presentation of their work to the Plenary. In the new Euro Corp, Proprietary Leadership Team would be able to market national brands, long-owned by Euro Corp to all European markets with resources never before available. The dialogue would continue, after the conference, between the Proprietary Leadership Team and the country organizations to achieve alignment and agreement. This meeting represented the kick-off of that process.

Leadership Team: debrief the day and prepare for tomorrow's wrap up
As was the daily practice, the Leadership Team convened at the end of the day to review the day's events and processes and decide if any modifications were necessary for the following day's agenda. The prime topic of discussion was the difficulty which the third country team had had with the country-simulation aimed at developing collaborative plans for a fictitious customer. The SVP of Country Y observed that the managers of the companies in his country had all been managers in ABC and the transition to a collaborative approach in working with customers and suppliers was new, and perhaps alien to them. It would take time for him to work with them to lead them in making the changes in how they worked—from competition to collaboration.

The Leadership Team also reviewed highlights of the week and prepared a brief presentation for the plenary for the next morning. They felt positive. The conference had been fun and productive. Relationships between and among people who had not known each other previously had gotten off on a good note. They also recognized and would communicate that the new Euro Corp had challenges. The new Supplier Management organization would have a difficult job in guiding the changes in behavior from competition to collaboration among the managers of the companies in the different companies. And the suppliers would also need to be educated in the new paradigms of Euro Corp. The larger ones would need to be shown that working with multiple companies within

Euro Corp would provide larger sales volumes than previously had been possible. They also recognized and would communicate that the roles and decision authorities were still not completely clear. The integration of ABC and Euro Corp would require more work in the coming months and as the Leadership Team they would guide that work.

The evening activity
A live band had been commissioned. And the party began. In addition to dancing, the highlight of the party was a sing-a-long led by the lead singer. The Louis Armstrong song, "What a wonderful world" was re-written and entitled "What a wonderful Euro Corp".

Day IV
23. September/ Friday
8:30

Reflections on Day III
The good feelings of party from the evening before spilled over to the morning.

Report back—reflections on the week by the Leadership Team
As they planned the evening before, the Leadership Team expressed their unified enthusiasm for the solid work and good fun of the conference. They also registered their awareness of and commitment to the continued work of making the integration of ABC and Euro Corp a success in the coming months. The difficult questions, particularly with regard to supplier management and further clarification of roles and decision authorities would be actively addressed.

Euro Corp Corporation Communications Plan: name change, etc.
The Communications Director next reported on the practical next steps planned for the change of company name: logos, business cards, etc. The Leadership Team was committed to making the changes expeditiously to assure clear messages to the market.

Preview of Next Steps in the Transformation Process
Picking up on the themes from Leadership Team's report and reflections on the week, Mary described in general terms the next steps the Leadership Team intended for the integration.

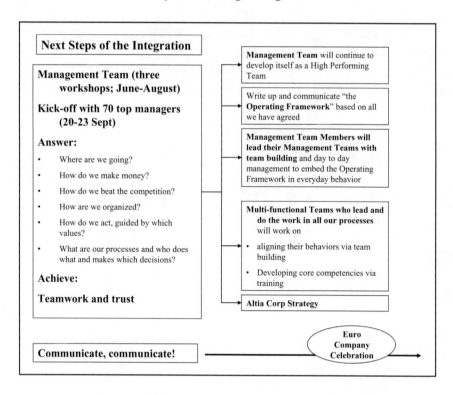

Feedback on the week and elevator speech

The feedback from the participants at the end of the meeting was thorough and enthusiastic, with some reservations. The leadership by Mary and the Leadership Team was acknowledged as a significant positive factor. The Leadership Team was seen as united and clear in the direction they were proposing for the new Euro Corp. The interactive activities on each aspect of the vision and operating framework permitted the participants to understand the elements well.

Significant questions remained concerning how the new Supplier Management organization would function. The interface with suppliers still seemed confusing to some. The details of the roles and decision making still were not completely clear even after the conclusion of the exercises which addressed these questions, although several reported that progress had been made.

There was also concern and lack of clarity on how and when precisely the divestiture of Euro Corp's logistics company, LOGI would occur.

Since quality logistics was a key factor in satisfying both suppliers and customers, the divestiture was a source of concern to many. If it would not be managed effectively and the logistics service levels were to fall, then significant business would be compromised.

The final feedback and mood of the meeting, when all 65 senior managements said their goodbyes was positive and energetic.

The Principles of Organizational Transformation and the case of the Leadership Conference; mobilizing the organization

The barriers to trust were considerable in this merger. During the period before Mary became CEO, the integration process was contentious and the management teams of the two companies had become alienated from each other. For the first several months of her tenure she formed her new management team from members of both companies. Over a series of meetings, she led the team to develop the operating framework, with my facilitation support, based on the Genesis Urgent Vision model while also building trust in the team through both the shared experience of designing the new organization and exercises such as personal story telling.

From the beginning, we employed the various tools of dialogue; in moments, such as confronting the misunderstandings of the early start up period; in meeting meetings of the management team and the Leadership Conference described above; and through the macro process of the series of meeting meetings that we evolved together. Step by step the team experienced the phases of dialogue and the process by which commitment was mobilized, first in the senior management team and next in the wider management circle of the top three levels of the company. Many managers reported during various feedback sessions, the process of designing and implementing a new organization through dialogue was a powerful (action) learning experience.

The boundaries of which level of management would address which dimension of the operating framework were clearly delineated; the senior management team presented the macro operating framework at the Leadership Conference and the next level managers were supported through facilitation to develop the more detailed aspects of the operating framework. The goals of the merger were clear throughout. The merged company would be able to leverage products and brands into new markets while managers had the challenge of operating in a broader arena, thus requiring each one to strengthen their individual capabilities. The approach required addressing the entire organizational system. The Leadership Conference addressed all sub-systems—the merger was an organization wide process.

Coda

As my partners and I have found repeatedly over the past twenty years, when leaders partner with facilitators who support them effectively in the processes of dialogue, constructive organizational change can happen. Performance can be improved over years, as was found in Arri's case in *Chapter 11, Long term improvement*. Major savings can be realized, as occurred in Michael's case in *Chapter 12, Globalization*. Priority, complex strategy can be developed in record time by the key implementation managers, the result in Kees's case in *Chapter 13, Accelerated Strategy Development*. And mergers can be implemented, that had nearly failed, as was evident in my case in *Chapter 14, Merger Integration*.

Dear Reader,
I hope this book has served to support your journey as a facilitator of organizational transformation.

Thomas F. Gross

Genesis Mission

Our mission is to partner with, support and coach leaders in the process of transforming their organizations to strengthen implementation and results. The process we employ involves and mobilizes people across the organization, from the leadership team to the front line, with shared understanding, ownership and commitment.

Genesis Values
Our values serve as guidelines for our behavior, with one another as partners and with our clients.

Partnership
We partner with our clients in a process of co-development to develop trust and empowerment, as we do internally, as Genesis partners.

Entrepreneurship
We strive for world-class performance through continuous action learning, grounded in reflection, innovative knowledge development and appropriate risk taking, whilst being continuously focused on implementation and delivery or results.

Integrity
We honor our commitments. If, for any reason, barriers prevent our capability to deliver on a commitment, we advise accordingly and whenever possible, in advance and search for alternative solutions.

Sustainability
We are committed to helping in the development of a more sustainable world. We promote the principles of sustainability economically, socially and environmentally.

References

- Argyris, Chris; <u>Knowledge for Action, *A Guide to Overcoming Barriers to Organizational Change*</u>; Jossey-Bass; 1993
- Argyris, Chris; <u>Organizational Traps: *Leadership, Culture, Organizational Design*</u>; Oxford University Press; 2010
- Argyris, Chris, <u>Theory in Practice: *Increasing Professional Effectiveness*</u>; Jossey Bass Higher and Adult Education Series; 1992
- Bohm, David; <u>On Dialogue</u>; Routledge; 1999
- Collins, James and Porras, Jerry, <u>Built to Last;</u> Harper Collins; 1994
- Gross, Thomas; <u>ICAR, Illusions, Crisis, Awareness, Realignment</u>; doctoral dissertation, Harvard University School of Education; 1980
- Gunderson, Lance and Holling, C.S.; <u>Panarchy, Understanding Transformations in Human and Natural Systems;</u> Island Press; 2002
- Isaacs, William; <u>Dialogue: The Art Of Thinking Together</u>; Doubleday; 1999
- Jane's Defense Weekly; a publication of the US Military; 2003
- Kuhn, Thomas; <u>The Structure of Scientific Revolutions</u>; The University of Chicago Press; 1962
- Pauw, Arri; <u>The Road Within</u>; Author House; 2010
- Lehrer, Jonah; <u>How we decide</u>; First Mariner Books; 2009
- Melnick, Joseph; Nevis, Sonia; Nevis, Edwin; "The Cycle of Experience"; Gestalt International Study Center; 2009
- Nevis, Edwin; <u>Organizational Consulting, A Gestalt Approach</u>; Gestalt Press, 1987
- Nevis, Sonia; "Rules for Self-organizing groups"; Gestalt International Study Center; 2009
- Nevis, S.; Backman, S.; Nevis, E.; "Connecting Strategic and Intimate Interactions: The Need for Balance"; Gestalt International Study Center; 2003
- Parens, Henri; Blum, Harold P.; Akhtar, Salmon; <u>The Unbroken Soul: Tragedy, Trauma and Resilience;</u> The Rowman and Littlefield Publishing Group; 2008
- Senge, Peter; <u>The Fifth Discipline;</u> Doubleday; 1990

- Stone, Douglass; Patton, Bruce; Heen, Shiela; <u>Difficult Conversations</u>; Viking Penguin; 1999
- Yankelovich, Daniel; <u>The Magic of Dialogue</u>; Touchstone; 1999
- Ulrich, Dave; Kerr, Steve; and Ashkenas, Ron; <u>*GE Work-Out: How to Implement GE's Revolutionary Method for Busting Bureaucracy & Attacking Organizational Problems*</u>; McGraw Hill, 2002
- Walker, Brian and Salt, David; <u>Resilience Thinking</u>, Island Press; 2006
- Wheatley, Margaret; <u>Finding our way: *Leadership for an Uncertain Time*</u>; Berrett-Koehler Publishers, Inc.; 2005
- Wolfram, Stephen; <u>A New Kind of Science</u>; Wolfram Media, Inc.; 2002

Biography

Tom Gross founded Genesis Consulting Group
in 1990 in Geneva, Switzerland. Contributing to
constructive change in large organizations and
institutions by facilitating dialogue has been his
career commitment for more than thirty years.
He has supported leaders and leadership teams
in designing and implementing change processes
across a wide spectrum of industries and countries
on all continents of the world. His clients have
included various headquarters of Fortune 500 corporations, other
international companies and non-governmental organizations devoted
to conservation, sustainable economic development, philanthropy and
international understanding.

He holds a B. A. in psychology from Princeton University, an M. A.
in organizational behavior from Yale University and an Ed. D. in
organizational behavior from Harvard University.

Summary

Mobilizing Commitment is written for facilitators of organizational transformation, including leaders as well as internal and external consultants. It presents a proven, practical guide of principles, methods and compelling case examples from Tom Gross's own practice and that of his partners on how organizational transformation is effectively facilitated through dialogue in multinational corporations all over the world. As Gross explains, *"The foundation of organizational transformation is a culture of trust that is enabled through relational dialogue and entails two-way feedback between individuals on their behavior. It is synergistic with strategic dialogue, the means for making sound decisions which are implemented and produce results. The facilitator supports the transformation process by facilitating moments of shared awareness, meetings of strategic and relational dialogue and macro processes across the entire organization to mobilize commitment."*